ModernScot

PATCHWORK

—— **Bold Quilts** ——
INSPIRED BY ICONIC TARTANS

KATHY ALLEN

C&T PUBLISHING

Text copyright © 2018 by Kathy Allen

Photography and artwork copyright © 2018 by C&T Publishing, Inc.

Publisher: Amy Marson

Creative Director: Gailen Runge

Editors: Karla Menaugh and Liz Aneloski

Technical Editor: Debbie Rodgers

Cover/Book Designer: April Mostek

Production Coordinator / Illustrator: Tim Manibusan

Production Editor: Jennifer Warren

Photo Assistant: Mai Yong Vang

Cover photography by Lucy Glover of C&T Publishing, Inc.

Book photography by Diane Pedersen and Mai Yong Vang of C&T Publishing, Inc., unless otherwise noted

Published by C&T Publishing, Inc., P.O. Box 1456, Lafayette, CA 94549

Library of Congress Cataloging-in-Publication Data

Names: Allen, Kathy, 1956- author.

Title: Modern Scot patchwork : bold quilts inspired by iconic tartans / Kathy Allen.

Description: Lafayette, CA : C&T Publishing, Inc., 2018. | Includes bibliographical references.

Identifiers: LCCN 2017039163 | ISBN 9781617455940 (soft cover)

Subjects: LCSH: Patchwork--Patterns. | Quilting--Patterns. | Tartans--Miscellanea.

Classification: LCC TT835 .A4563 2018 | DDC 746.46/041--dc23

LC record available at https://lccn.loc.gov/2017039163

Printed in China

10 9 8 7 6 5 4 3 2 1

Dedication

To my husband and companion, Frank, whose tangible love,

friendship, and encouragement have provided the bedrock

and strength upon which my life is built.

Acknowledgments

More than anyone, Anelie Belden has led me to where I am in the fabric arts. She taught me how to sew, taught me how to quilt, taught me how to make garments, and most of all, taught me to love the machine. She is an exceptional teacher. She is an extraordinary artist and designer.

In the creation of this book, Anelie provided insight into what is easy for quilting students to understand, and then she checked the math—evidence of true friendship! Using her experience in quilting, designing quilt patterns, and as an author, she checked my instructions to make sure they were both accurate and understandable. But more than anything else, she gave me the confidence that I could design. For all this and more, I give my most heartfelt thanks and gratitude.

I want to also thank my quilting class girls—Cheryl Allen, Nancy Gebauer, Nancy Hardy, Angel LeSage, Laurel Lissner, Olive Lissner, Trisha Rogers, and Lola Thomas— for helping me make the quilts that are on display in this book and for helping me learn how to teach. Without them, I couldn't have met my deadlines. By making the quilts, they found the mistakes: both those hidden away and those glaringly obvious.

Special thanks to Sydney Wright for her ever present assistance and youthful insight. Also invaluable to this endeavor were Beverly Ortiz for binding with perfection, Linda DeRosia for preparing beautiful embroidered labels, and Shannon Ryan-Freeman for her excellent longarm quilting skills.

Finally, I want to thank the people of Scotland, whose rich history and beautiful country have served as an inspiration for these quilting patterns. The world has benefited from their artistry and meticulous weaving skills, which have created so many lovely, lovely plaids and tartans.

Contents

Introduction　6

History of the Tartan　7

Choosing Fabric　10

Basic Quiltmaking Techniques　14

How to Build a Tartan Design　16

Gallery　104

Fabric Organization Worksheet　110

Bibliography / About the Author　111

The Projects

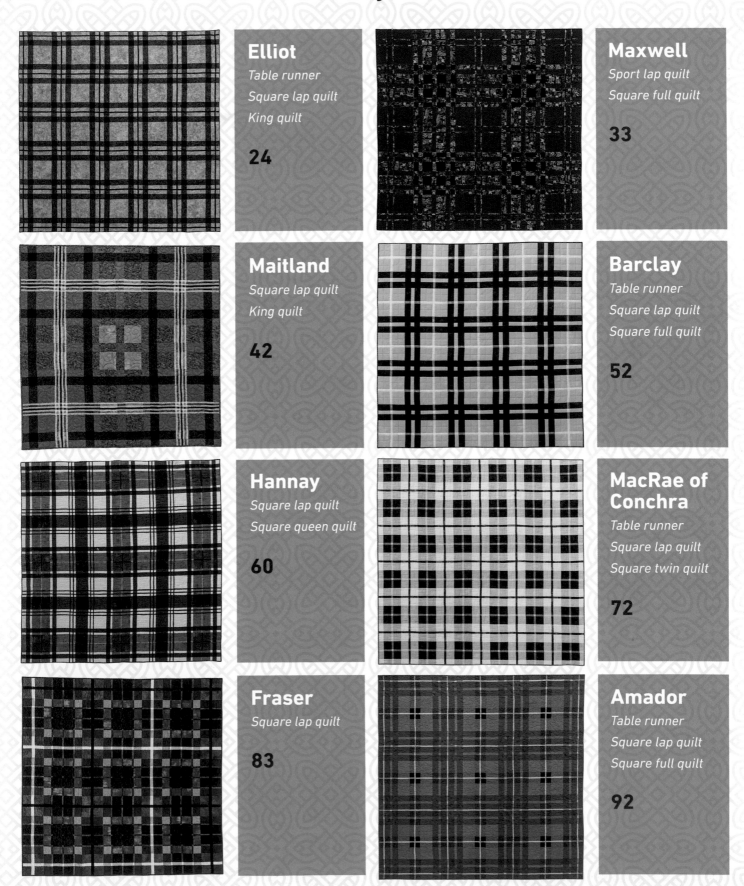

Elliot
Table runner
Square lap quilt
King quilt

24

Maxwell
Sport lap quilt
Square full quilt

33

Maitland
Square lap quilt
King quilt

42

Barclay
Table runner
Square lap quilt
Square full quilt

52

Hannay
Square lap quilt
Square queen quilt

60

MacRae of Conchra
Table runner
Square lap quilt
Square twin quilt

72

Fraser
Square lap quilt

83

Amador
Table runner
Square lap quilt
Square full quilt

92

Introduction

When traveling through Scotland, whether it be to historic Edinburgh, the rolling hills of Aberdeen, or the mountains surrounding Fort William, it's hard to escape the visual impact of the dominant pattern we call plaid. It's in the wallpaper, it's on the carpets, and it's in the clothing—and the variety of tartans seems endless.

Made famous by the Harry Potter movie depictions of the Hogwart Express, the Glenfinnan Viaduct is located at the head of Loch Shiel between Fort William and Mallaig. Glenfinnan is said to be the origin of the second Jacobite uprisings, started in 1746.

Photo by PhotoSpin.com/Achim Prill

History of the Tartan

Although commonly associated with the Highland clans of Scotland, the design pattern known as *tartan* or *plaid* is much older. It was used in ancient cultures including the pre-Celtic cultures of central Europe of the eighth century BC (what we call the Iron Age), Western China from 1800 BC, and Scandinavia.

The earliest tartan in Britain is known as the Falkirk tartan, found in a jar of Roman coins just north of Scotland's Antonine Wall. Some do not consider it a proper tartan because its design is more of a check than a plaid; nevertheless, it is remarkable that a piece of ancient fabric with distinct color striations has held up despite the progression of time. There are theories about how a piece of tartan cloth found its way into a pot of Roman gold. My favorite theory surmises that a drunken Scot stole the gold, hid it, and forgot the hiding place. The Falkirk tartan is on display in the National Museum of Scotland.

The association of a particular tartan with a particular locality and clan wasn't specifically documented until 1703. Martin Martin described a tartan as a fine-wool cloth carefully woven by clans-women to create exact patterns. A person's place of residence was known immediately by the pattern in their clothing, he said. Because of the time it took to learn the skillful weaving of tartan, it is assumed by some that the Highland clan association with specific patterns was probably started sometime in the fourteenth century.

No other fabric has had such a prominent role in the history and politics of a country or has been written about so often in poems and historical novels. The rivalry between England and Scotland was based primarily on the ruling English royal family, the Hanovers, maintaining power and the Highland Scots's desire to put a Stuart back on the throne. The Highland Scots started to wear the tartan not just as their clothing but also to show their discontent and enmity with England. The tartan was the symbol of patriotic fervor. The Lowland Scots, especially the women of the aristocracy, followed suit and started to wear the tartan around 1707 to show their disapproval of the Act of Union; new tartans were designed to represent these Lowland clans.

Highland dancer wearing a modern-style kilt with Prince Charlie jacket, kilt with sporran, and ghillie brogues

Photo by PhotoSpin.com/ Valentyna Chukhlyebova

Sir Walter Scott, the beloved poet and playwright, helped propel the prestige of the tartan and even made it fashionably chic, with lines in such battle poems as "Elspeth's Ballad": "Their tartans they were waving wide."

In 1746, after the now-famous bloody battle at Culloden, the triumphant English passed the Disarming Act and the Dress Act, making it law that the Scottish could not own weapons nor wear the tartan. However, those Scots who supported the Hanovers were allowed to continue having their portraits made wearing the traditional tartan kilts. (I think we can safely assume that there was some disobedience of this law by those who could afford a way of hiding their forbidden garments.)

The great tragedy of the Dress Act was that many of the old tartan patterns were lost forever, as were the special skills of the clanswomen who weaved the wool. A few tartan patterns survived, either because they were recorded in paintings or because pieces of cloth were hidden away.

The return of the tartan as an article of clothing for all began when the Dress Act was repealed in 1782. In 1800 there were a handful of patterns, and by 1820 almost 150. Research began in earnest to find and restore the ancient tartan patterns in 1822, when Sir Walter Scott arranged for King George IV to visit Edinburgh. The Scottish clans put on a glorious pageant for the elderly king, with their tartans center stage. Today 5,000 to 7,000 tartans are registered.

Throughout this period of the early to mid-1700s, the tartan found its way to the New World. After the first Jacobite rebellion of 1715, the rebels were put to death or imprisoned. In 1717, the surviving rebels were punished by being shipped to Virginia to serve seven-year terms as indentured servants. Many of these prisoners liked America and wrote to their families to join them once their service was complete. When the English realized that being

Photo by PhotoSpin.com/Darren Green

Eilean Donan ("Island of Donan") Castle is the ancestral home of Clan MacKenzie and Clan MacRae of Conchra. It was destroyed in 1719 after the first Jacobite war as punishment for the clan's participation in the Jacobite rebellion. Eilean Donan Castle was rebuilt by the MacRaes in the early twentieth century and is used today for films and weddings.

----

moved—at cost to the government—was not viewed negatively, different punishments had to be found.

The next great immigration to the New World came in the 1760s. The Jacobite wars had impoverished the clans, and America was viewed as an opportunity away from starvation. Once again, the Scottish immigrants took the tartan with them to their new homes. By the time the American Revolution started, 6 percent of the population in the 13 colonies were born in Scotland. Interestingly, most of them were loyalists—especially the Highlanders! This was primarily due to financial interests rather than political ones, by way of the ever-important trade of tobacco and cotton: one leg of the transatlantic trade route that also included rum and slaves. But not all Scots were loyal to the English crown. 19 (one-third) of the 56 signers of the American Declaration of Independence were either born in Scotland or their parents were.

National Tartan Day, April 6, celebrates the historic link between Scotland and the New World, particularly Argentina, Australia, Canada, and the United States. Nova Scotia (New Scotland) still has villages where Gaelic is spoken as it was when the Scots immigrated there. The largest of the Highland games outside Scotland is celebrated each fall in Pleasanton, California.

Bagpipers from several different clans in modern highland-style kilts on parade

What is Tartan? What is Plaid?

In the United States, we use the terms *tartan* and *plaid* as though they were interchangeable. In Scotland, however, tartan refers to the woolen, latticed fabric that is used for clothing, and plaid refers to how the fabric is used—the large broad cloth that is worn and wrapped around like a skirt, with the excess fabric slung across the shoulder. In Gaelic, *plaide* means "blanket."

The modern kilt, also made of tartan fabric, was invented in 1720 by a Quaker from Lancashire. His design made it easier for his Scottish workers to work, as the traditional belted broadcloth was bulky and cumbersome. Instead of a single piece of fabric (plaid), the tartan was cut and used in two pieces: a small piece for the skirt, or *kilt*, and a second piece slung over the shoulders as an accessory, which is now called *plaid*. Hence, the project designs in this book may have been inspired by the pattern of traditional tartans, but the final products are appropriately referred to as plaids!

Tartans are made by interweaving the colored thread from the vertical *warp* with the horizontal *weft*. When a weft color crosses the same warp color, the intersecting area stays the same color because the intersecting threads are all the same color. When the weft color crosses a different warp color, the intersecting threads create a new color: a merge of the two intersecting colors. The total number of colors in a tartan increases quadratically from the number of bases. So two bases result in three colors, three bases result in six colors, four bases result in ten colors, and so on. The more colors, the more subdued the pattern becomes.

Tartans have been designed and used not just for Scottish clans but also for countries, businesses, and events. Eighteen U.S. states have adopted official tartans, including California, Louisiana, Georgia, and Hawaii.

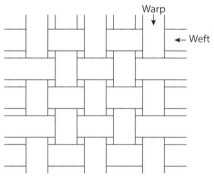

The warp thread is intersected above—and then alternatively below—by the weft thread, creating color blocks of either the base color or the merge color.

The patterns in this book are loose interpretations of traditional Scottish clan tartans, except the tartan Amador (page 92), which I designed to honor the area in which I live. I chose the tartans based on their ease of conversion to "quiltability." There may be many Scottish traditionalists who are horrified at the thought of an American modeling a quilt pattern on something that they hold so dear. I hope they can forgive such brazen audacity and understand that it is for the love of the design that I have used their tartans as inspiration for quilts.

Choosing Fabric

Color selection is a personal choice. I often select colors that are coincident with the traditional patterns of the tartans, but I have tried to show some projects that move away from the traditional base colors. As modern quilt styles, these patterns lend themselves to many of the modern fabrics that reflect both the urban and masculine influence; however, Civil War and 1930s reproductions, as well as novelty and traditional tone-on-tone fabrics, also make for interesting quilts.

Modern, Ancient, and Reproduction Color Schemes

Traditional tartan colors fall into three categories:

Modern: The colors are dark and strong, with blue barely distinguishable from black.

Ancient: The colors are light and almost pastel, intended to represent the colors that would result by using natural dyes such as bark, berries, or moss.

Reproduction: The colors are muted, meant to represent the colors of a fragment dug up in the peat of Culloden Moor—generally brownish. Reproduction can also mean fabric colors from the early 1800s.

The original tartans were made from the natural colors of the wool—black, brown, and creamy white. Later tartan wools were dyed with berries, leaves, lichens, flowers, and bark, with urine used as a source of ammonia to intensify the color. To set the color, the wool would be washed in iron fixative collected from the black peat bogs.

Base Fabrics and Merge Fabrics

In this book, fabric falls into one of two categories:

Base fabrics: The colors that form the basis of the tartan. They are usually red, yellow, green, blue, black, or white but are occasionally purple or orange.

Merge fabrics: The colors that form when two base fabrics meet

For base fabrics, I often use solids or tone-on-tone prints. I sometimes like to use fabrics that may have a print in addition to the dominant color to give the final quilt depth, movement, or dimensionality.

For merge fabrics, you have several options:

Use a fabric that incorporates the two base colors that are being merged, such as a red-and-black print when the base fabrics are red and black.

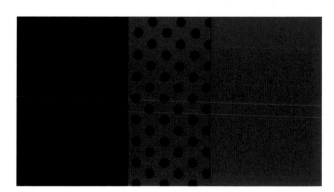

Choose a fabric that blends the two colors, such as a dark red when the base fabrics are red and black. In the case of merging yellow and blue, the merge fabric would be green.

Ignore the rules altogether. In this example, I chose a merge fabric with a dark red background, but it barely shows behind the busy multicolor print. Your choices could be even more unusual. My niece Sydney Wright made a quilt in which the merge fabric for the bases of white and purple was lime green! When you choose unusual merge fabrics, you may not achieve the effect of one color being woven into another, but the contrast in colors will create a beautiful design.

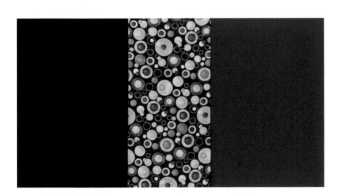

TIP **Solids or Prints?** Using solids or tone-on-tone prints will give you the most traditional look of woven fabric. But if your quilt has some large squares and rectangles, you can use novelty fabrics with fun designs and themes to still achieve a plaid pattern. See the *Hannay* square lap quilt (page 61) and the *Maxwell* square full quilt (page 33) for examples of quilts that incorporated novelty fabrics.

Color and Value

Color is important, but value is more important in these projects. Why? Because it is through *value* (the lightness or the darkness of a fabric) that the perception of color is presented. It is through value that the design will show itself. In these projects, it is more important that there is a variety of values than a visually pleasing color scheme. You will find that you need to use some low-value colors in your quilts, as they are critical to the success of these designs.

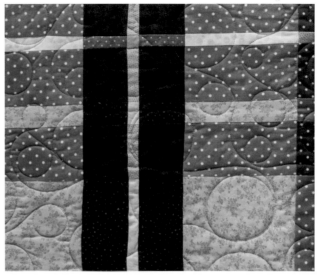

In the *Amador* square lap quilt (page 93), the colors of the adjacent greens range from blue-green to olive green, but they work well together because the differences in value make the pattern stand out.

Fabric with a low value looks dark, sometimes even black; fabric with a high value has a pure, fully saturated color. One is not better than the other. *Both* are needed in these projects to bring out the design of the quilt. A quilt with only medium-value fabrics will not show off the design, but if fabrics of very low and very high value are added to the mix (even in a small amount), the result is a more powerful representation of the quilt design.

As an example of the importance of value, consider the impact of the thin stripes running through the *Maitland* quilts (page 42). It is the extreme contrast of values that makes this pattern so stunning.

An interesting aspect of value to consider is its relative impact. A medium-value fabric will look dark against a light-value fabric but look light against a dark-value fabric. Keep this in mind as you choose the fabrics for your quilts.

The impact of the light-value stripes running through the darker-value fabric makes a dramatic impact in the *Maitland* quilts (page 42).

Black Fabric

Most tartans have black (or a very, very low-value blue or green) in them, even if it's just a tiny sliver that runs inconspicuously through one of the main colors. Because black often defines the pattern, different black styles may impact the overall look of the quilt. Many times you may not want an actual black but a very low-value color, such as a blue or green; this is especially true when using hand-dyed fabrics such as batiks. The *Elliot* king quilt (page 24) is a good example of this. Sometimes you will want a fabric that is dominantly black but has an additional color or design—or both. These could add motion or depth to the quilt.

Different black fabrics will give different characteristics to your project. That's because the pigments and dyes specific to the fabrics have different light-absorption properties. Some black fabrics have a shininess to them, making them look more silver gray than black. Other black fabrics look like dark gray when placed next to a darker black. Some black fabrics are cool and some are warm. If the black fabric has a pattern, it will have the effect of adding texture or even movement to the overall design.

When selecting a black fabric for your project, audition it first. Black may be a very small part of the overall quilt, but it makes a strong impact.

Washing Fabric

I am a firm believer in washing fabric before using it—and not just batiks and other hand-dyed fabrics (which tend to leach and can ruin a finished quilt)— but any fabric. The main reason is because of formaldehyde. Formaldehyde is used to bind color to fabric, provide that stiffness we all love, and serve as a fire retardant; it is also used to prevent mildew during shipping. That odor that we all associate with fabric stores is the formaldehyde in the fabric. The problem is that this highly toxic, colorless gas has been linked to skin irritation and allergies in some people. It is also a known carcinogen for those with high and prolonged exposure, which quilters generally are not. Washing the fabric will eliminate some, but not all, of the chemical. This is not meant to scare quilters away from quilting but merely to serve as a sound rationale for washing fabric before using it (and washing clothes before wearing them).

Formaldehyde is not the only chemical in our cotton fabric. The entire process of taking natural cotton from the plant to become fabric is filled with chemicals. N-Propyl Mercaptan (a derivative of sulfur that has a pungent smell) is sprayed on the plants to prevent boll weevil. When the cotton plants are harvested, mercaptans are used again—this time as an exfoliant to make the leaves fall off the plants and to make the harvest of the cotton fiber easier. A chemical stiffener is added during weaving to prevent warp in the yarn. The raw fabric is then bleached to remove all of the chemicals used thus far. Afterward, the fabric is mercerized with caustic soda that makes the yarn swell and then shrink so that the dye will adhere to the fabric better and the final product will have a silken luster. Finally, formaldehyde is added to give the fibers stability.

Maybe this is more information than you wanted to know on the preparation of cotton fabric. But knowing how fabric is prepared benefits quilters because they know how to treat and take care of their quilts, as well as appreciate the overall process. I compare it to knowing about the grape varietal when drinking wine. There are so many factors that influence a final wine product, and the same can be said about fabric.

If you like to work with stiff fabric like I do, wash it first; then put some liquid starch in the rinse cycle. You will get rid of the toxic chemicals but still have a bit of that stiffness that is so pleasant to work with.

Basic Quiltmaking Techniques

For these tartan-inspired quilts, three critical sewing issues are stitch length, ¼″ seam accuracy, and pinning.

Stitch Length

I recommend shortening the stitch length for the projects in this book because the quadruple- and triple-strip sets will be subcut into segments. If your stitch is too long, the thread will release and the edges of the triplets and quartets will come undone. This is especially true for triplets and quartets that are only 1″ wide. The main disadvantage to shortening the stitch length is that it makes it difficult to rip out stitches. If I make a mistake and have enough fabric, I sometimes just make a new double-strip or triple-strip set.

Depending on the type of sewing machine you have, stitch length is measured one of two ways:

- The actual length of the stitch in millimeters (mm)
- Stitches per inch (SPI)—how many stitches there are in 1″

The average stitch length for medium-weight fabric is 2.5–3 mm or 10–12 SPI. The usual default setting for most sewing machines is 2.4 mm. I tend to use 1.6 mm or 17 SPI.

¼″ Seam Accuracy

I find it rather hypocritical on my part to discuss seam accuracy because, frankly, my seams often vary from crooked country lanes to ten-lane superhighways. Nevertheless, making accurate ¼″ seams is crucial in these projects—especially those with ½″ final strip widths—if the illusion of crisscrossing strips is to be created. What is most important is that the ¼″ seams are consistently the same size.

One of the best ways to get an accurate ¼″ seam is to use a ¼″ foot and use the built-in guide as you sew. But keep in mind that different machines have different ¼″ seams. You can test the accuracy of your technique and machine by sewing together 4 strips 1½″ × 5″. The final width of this multi-strip should be 4½″ wide.

If you are new to sewing, time and experience will eventually help you make seams that are consistent. However, even imperfect seams can result in beautiful intersections if you pin before you sew.

Pinning

Whenever two seams meet, pin them to ensure that the fabric doesn't move when the presser foot moves over them. The pin should be placed after the seam. Do not sew over the pin, as the needle may nick the pin and both may break, potentially flying off into the air toward your eyes. Take the pin out after crossing the seam but before reaching the pin.

Place pins at each seam intersection, after the seam. If the seams of two pieces are pressed in opposite directions, the seams will "nest" together, making it even easier to create neat corners.

Fabric Quantity

Each project includes yardage requirements based on 40″ usable width of fabric. If you are planning to make your quilt a little larger or if you are wondering if a particular strip of fabric from your stash is large enough, refer to this table to remind yourself how many inches are in popular yardage cuts.

For example, if you need 2 strips 2½″ wide (5″ total), as well as 12 strips 1″ wide (12″ total), you would need 17″ of fabric. In that case, ½ yard might be sufficient, but it would be wiser to go with ¾ yard to account for shrinkage, fabric that is off-grain, or cutting inaccuracies.

YARDAGE	INCHES
1 yard	36″
¾ yard	27″
½ yard	18″
¼ yard	9″
⅛ yard	4½″

Check the width of your fabrics; if you have any fabrics less than 40″, you may need more strips (and more yardage).

TIP **Buy Yardage Rather Than Fat Quarters** I highly recommend that you buy yardage, cutting all strips across the full width of fabric rather than from fat quarters. All instructions are based on strips cut across the width of fabric that has at least 40″ usable width. For wider strips and larger components, you will not be able to cut the same number of pieces from a fat quarter. Save fat quarters for some of the less prominent fabrics in a project, when you need to cut just a few components. If all you have are fat quarters, follow the directions but cut twice as many strips.

Troubleshooting Fabric Quantity

Many of these patterns require making a full triple- or quadruple-strip set just to cut out two to six tiny components, leaving a lot of unused material in the strip set.

At times, I have had the perfect fabric but not the sufficient quantity for both the large and small strips. I have been known to rip out leftover 3½″ fabric from the unused portion of a triple-

strip set and cut it into 2 strips 1¼″ for a different triple-strip set. If I know ahead of time that I don't have enough fabric to do it the way the instructions call for, I always cut the big pieces first, knowing that I will have leftovers that I can cut smaller later. Sometimes fabric selection requires ingenuity and the willingness to unsew to get it just right.

How to Build a Tartan Design

This very simple technique is so easy that even beginners can make beautiful tartan-inspired quilts! There are just six steps:

STEP 1 Cut strips of each fabric at the size indicated × the width of fabric.

STEP 2 Sew the strips together to create double-strip sets.

STEP 3 Sew double-strip sets together to create quadruple-strip sets, or sew on a third strip to create a triple-strip set.

STEP 4 Subcut the quadruple- and triple-strip sets into segments to create quartets or triplets and connectors.

STEP 5 Sew quartets, triplets, and/or connectors (strips of a designated dimension) end to end to create rows.

STEP 6 Sew the rows together in the indicated order to finish the quilt top.

For each tartan, I have included a diagram of a complete pattern with colors designated by letter. The numbers refer to the finished width or length of each piece.

NOTE: Dimensions

The diagrams show the finished dimensions of each piece, which are the measurements of the piece after the quilt has been sewn together. The cutting directions add ½″ to both the width and length to account for ¼″ seam allowances.

Keeping track of the fabrics used for the many colors is essential, as several of these quilts use quite a few fabrics. Use the fabric organization worksheet (page 110) to keep track of your fabric swatches.

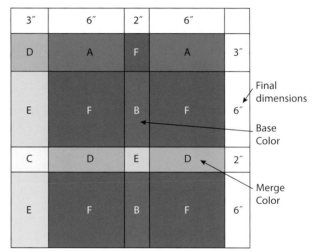

This sample diagram shows the base colors of red (A), black (B), and yellow (C).

Wherever a base color in the weft meets the same color in the warp, the intersecting square or rectangle stays the same color. However, whenever a base color crosses a different base color, the intersecting square or rectangle needs to be a *merge color*: a cross between the two intersecting colors. The merge colors in this sample are red/yellow merge (D), black/yellow merge (E), and black/red merge (F). The finished dimensions of the weft rows and warp columns are shown in the top row and right column.

For each project, I have included color-coded cutting tables that coordinate with the colors in the quilt construction diagrams.

STEP 1 Cut Strips of Each Fabric

The first table for each project tells you how many strips to cut for each fabric and how wide to cut each one, depending on your project size. You will use these strips to make strip sets, from which you will cut quartets, triplets, or other pieced segments. The table is color coded to match the project's construction diagram, and it lists both the color-designated letter and the full color name. It is the only table that links the color name with its letter designate. An example of this table is below.

TIP **Directional Fabric** If your fabric is directional and you want to keep the design elements oriented in the same direction, you may need additional strips and fabric. I truly believe that you can ignore the direction of your fabric pattern and end up with beautiful results. In quilts that have inverse pieces and connectors, the fabric often ends up facing in all four directions in a balanced way. Value is more important than color and direction.

FABRIC		STRIP WIDTH	NUMBER OF STRIPS TO CUT		
			Table runner	Square lap quilt	Square full quilt
Yellow (A)		5½″	6	10	18
		2″	2	4	7
Black (B)		3″	2	4	6
White (C)		1½″	1	1	1
Yellow/white merge (D)		5½″	2	2	2
		2″	1	1	1
		1½″	3	5	9
Yellow/black merge (E)		5½″	2	5	6
		3″	4	8	14
		2″	1	0	6
Black/white merge (F)		3″	2	2	2
		1½″	1	2	3
Binding		2½″	6	8	9

Cutting the Strips

1. Fold the fabric selvage to selvage, but let the fold be natural and fall on the grain. Because of the nature of the weave, sometimes the natural fold will be a little catawampus to the selvage. That's okay. In fact, it's more common than not. I usually find myself having to refold (and re-iron) the fabric as I cut more and more of it because the two edges get too far apart. Don't let a need for perfection make you force the selvages to match. Your final quilt will look much better if you ignore the fabric imperfections and always cut on the grain.

2. Always press the fabric before cutting to get a nice sharp fold.

TIP Check the back of the folded fabric. Sometimes a wrinkle will form on the fabric underneath, and it gets ironed in. When this happens, the strip will have a pronounced jog in it, making it unusable.

3. Place the pressed fold on a measured horizontal line on a self-healing cutting board. Use the rotary ruler and cutter to create a straight edge on the left side of the fabric (or the right, if you are left-handed).

4. Align the straight edge of the fabric with the ruler marking for your desired strip width. Cut!

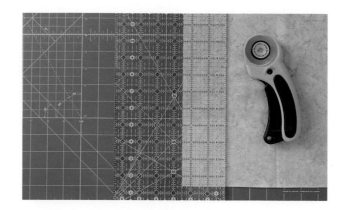

STEP 2 Sew the Strips Together to Create Double-Strip Sets

When sewing strips together and pressing the seams, try not to pull or stretch the strips. Doing so will make the final multi-strips bow, resulting in crooked and uneven quartets and triplets.

Press carefully to keep double-strip sets straight.

STEP 3 Create Quadruple- and Triple-Strip Sets

Sew two double-strip sets together to make a quadruple-strip set, or add a single strip to a double-strip set to create a triple-strip set. Try to sew the second round of strips in the opposite direction from the original double-strip sets. This will balance out any potential stretching and bowing.

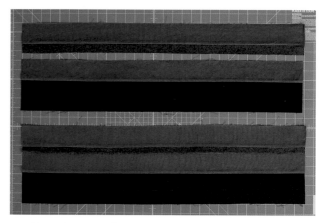

STEP 4 Subcut Quartets, Triplets, and Connectors

To see how many triplets, quartets, or other pieces to subcut from your strip sets, see the lists in each project. The illustration with each list shows the order of the fabric in the strip sets. The list shows the identifier number for each quartet or triplet

(for example, triplet 2), the width to cut the quartets and triplets (for example, 2½″), and the quantity of quartets and triplets to cut. You will use these quartets and triplets to make rows later.

See the example below:

TRIPLE-STRIP SET 2

Make 1 strip set for the square lap quilt or 3 for the square full quilt. Subcut triplets 2 and 7.

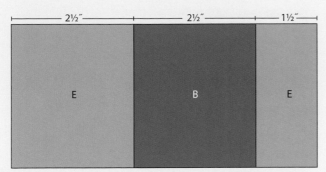

This illustration shows the order and size of strips that make up the triple-strip set.

Square lap quilt

⌐ Triplet 7: 2 segments 6½″ wide

⌐ Triplet 2: 8 segments 2½″ wide

Square full quilt

⌐ Triplet 7: 8 segments 6½″ wide

⌐ Triplet 2: 12 segments 2½″ wide

◆ **TIP** **Conserving Fabric** When the instructions call for you to make more than one strip set, subcut all the larger triplet, quartet, or connector components first; then subcut the smaller segments from the remaining portions of the strip sets.

For example, in the list above, you need 8 segments 6½″ wide for triplet 7 in the square full quilt. You can cut 6 of the 6½″ segments from a 40″ strip set. Cut the 2 remaining 6½″ segments from another strip set; then use the remainder to subcut 10 of the 2½″ segments. Cut the last 2 segments from a third strip. If you cut all the smaller segments first, you may not have long enough strip sets left to cut all the larger segments.

Cutting the Quartets and Triplets ---

With the bottom strip of the triple- or quadruple-strip set aligned with a horizontal line of the cutting board, subcut segments at the width listed for each piece. If the triple- or quadruple-strip set is a bit catawampus, straighten the edge frequently with a clean cut. (You will waste a bit of fabric doing this, so frequent clean cuts may require you to make additional strip sets. It will be worth it to keep your segments square.)

◆ **TIP** **Label the Quartets and Triplets!** Making tartan quilts requires lots of different components. Be sure to label them and keep them organized!

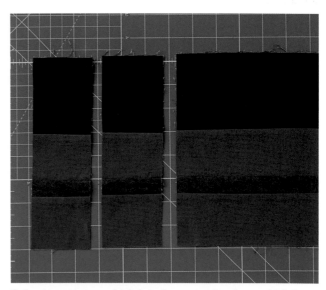

Subcut quartets and triplets from quadruple- and triple-strip sets.

Connectors

Some of the projects will have connectors, which are single fabric rectangles used in between quartets and triplets. A table describing the strip size, connector size, and number to cut is included for these projects. The fabric strips used for connectors are included in the cutting table; cut the connectors from the strips left over after you have made the quadruple- and triple-strip sets.

The table below shows that this project has 4 types of connectors, numbered 1 through 4. For example, to make connector 1, you would use the leftover 2½″ blue (B) strips to subcut rectangles 10½″ long. You would need 36 of these connectors in the king quilt.

FABRIC		CONNECTOR NUMBER	STRIP WIDTH	SUBCUT SEGMENTS THIS WIDE	QUANTITY		
					Table runner	Square lap quilt	King quilt
Blue (B)		4	10½″	10½″	3	6	15
		1	2½″	10½″	8	16	36
Red/blue merge (E)		2	1¼″	10½″	4	8	18
Blue/black merge (F)		3	3½″	10½″	6	12	30

STEP 5 Sew Quartets, Triplets, and/or Connectors Together to Create Rows

To create rows, sew the triplets and quartets end to end. Some patterns have connectors. Many of the quartets and triplets are directional and can be placed in the quilt in two directions—indicated by "inverse" in the construction table. Some triplets, such as those in the *Barclay* and *MacRae* quilts, are palindromes (reading the same forward and backward), so they don't have an inverse direction.

This is an example of a quartet that can be placed in two directions.

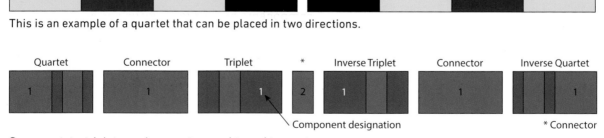

Quartet   Connector   Triplet   *   Inverse Triplet   Connector   Inverse Quartet

Component designation

* Connector

Sew quartets, triplets, and connectors end to end to create rows.

In some instances, specifically in making multi-rows, you will need to sew the components together side to side rather than end to end.

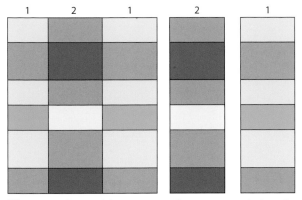

When creating multi-rows, sew the components together side to side rather than end to end. Remember to pin!

The repeating pattern in tartans means that there will be many copies of the same row within the quilt top. To make the piecing easier, use chain piecing for these quilts. In the sample Row Types table below, there are only four types of rows, and these are designated by alphabetical letters.

The Row Types table for each project size describes the order that the quartets, triplets, and connectors are sewn together to create the different types of rows. In the sample table, you would make the D rows by sewing the following components together end-to-end: triplet 6, inverse triplet 2, quartet 6, connector 2, inverse quartet 6, triplet 2, and inverse triplet 6.

Row Types

ROW TYPE AND NUMBER TO MAKE	TRIPLET	INVERSE TRIPLET	QUARTET	CONNECTOR	INVERSE QUARTET	TRIPLET	INVERSE TRIPLET
A: Make 8.	7	3	7	3	7	3	7
B: Make 4.	8	4	8	4	8	4	8
C: Make 3.	5	1	5	1	5	1	5
D: Make 3.	6	2	6	2	6	2	6

STEP 6 Sew the Rows Together

Once you have sewn all the different types of rows, you can sew them together to finish the quilt. The row types are listed in order from top to bottom in the assembly diagram, which will help you see the construction for your quilt size. Press the seams of adjacent rows in opposite directions to encourage the seams to nest. To ensure a perfect and clean fit, you should also pin every single seam intersection.

The patterns in these tartan-inspired quilts show up best if the rows and columns match.

Once you understand how to count the number of components needed for a particular project size, as well as the order of their placement, it is easy to modify the size of the final quilt to make it either larger or smaller. You can even change what is considered the pattern center by adding or subtracting components.

Multi-Pattern Quilts

Most of these tartan-inspired quilt projects are easy to make if you are making a single-pattern quilt—one repetition of the pattern. However, the more patterns that are put together, the more complex the quilt becomes. For instance, *Maxwell*, which has only three colors and is straightforward when making the single-pattern sport lap quilt, gets more complex when making a four-pattern square full quilt.

Some Last Comments

Chain Piecing

Feeding units into the sewing machine one right after another in "chains" makes the task of creating rows go much faster.

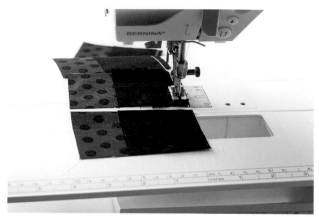

When chain piecing, it is unnecessary to cut the thread between sewing units.

Pressing

Except for the creation of the quartets and triplets, I wait to press until each row is complete so that I can press adjacent rows in alternate directions, which creates a nesting effect where the seams meet. Because of the previous pressing of the strip sets for quartets and triplets, you will have to do some "back pressing" where the direction changes from the original.

Quilt Size

It is easy to adjust the size of these quilts by adding or subtracting rows following the pattern. If you add just a few rows instead of a full pattern, though, you may change the overall look of the quilt. That's fine; it's your quilt!

With the exception of the table runners, all of the quilts in these projects are square. These square quilts will fit your beds a little differently, covering more of the side drop between the top of the bed and the floor but perhaps a bit shorter in length than standard sizes. I've named them "square twin," or "square full" so you can see which bed size they coordinate with. I created a new quilt size in these projects—the sport lap quilt. At 48″ × 48″, these small throws are perfect for sporting events.

Backing

After you have pieced the top, you often will have a lot of unused triple- and quadruple-strip sets. I like to sew these together with the main backing fabric to make an interesting, modern pattern on the back. This is something I learned from my first quilting teacher, Anelie Belden, to both conserve fabric and make something beautiful.

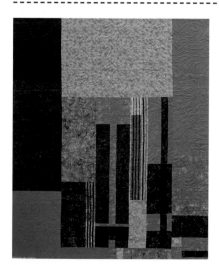

Detail of the *Maitland* king quilt (page 43), showing the backing

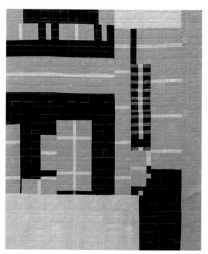

Detail of the *Barclay* square full quilt (page 52), showing the backing

Detail of the *MacRae of Conchra* square twin quilt (page 72), showing the backing

Quilting

Many of the quilts I make in these designs are quilted by stitching-in-the-ditch—that is, following the pattern directly. However, free-motion quilting can add a beautiful dimensionality to the final product.

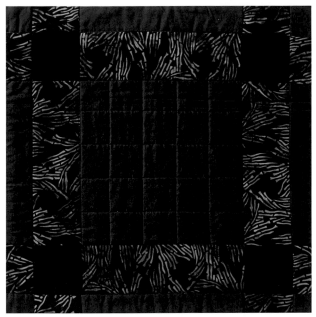

The stitch-in-the-ditch and straight-line quilting of this *Elliot* table runner (page 25) keep the focus on the pattern.

The swirly patterns of the gold fabric are echoed in the free-motion quilting of the *Barclay* square lap quilt (page 53).

Free-motion quilting adds to the overall design of the *Hannay* square queen quilt (page 60).

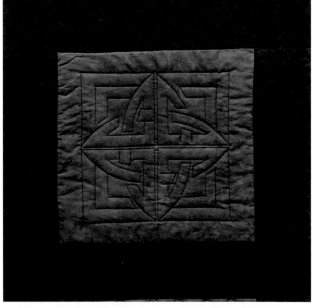

Large spaces lend themselves to specialty quilting, such as a Celtic knot in the *Elliot* square lap quilt (page 25).

Binding

Most of these quilts have no borders, so I like wider binding that frames the design. For standard binding, I cut 2½″ strips and sew the binding to the quilt with a generous ¼″ seam. For even wider binding, I often cut strips at 3″ and sew the binding to the quilt with a ½″ seam.

Enjoy making tartan-inspired quilts!

Skill Level:
BEGINNER

Elliot

Elliot king quilt, 108½″ × 108½″, made by Kathy Allen, quilted by Shannon Ryan-Freeman, 2017

There are two distinct patterns over the solid blue background—the thick black-and-blue stripes and the thin red stripes that pop. This quilt is made completely with batiks selected from the traditional color palette but from different hues. The nature of the blue batiks gives this quilt a water-like quality.

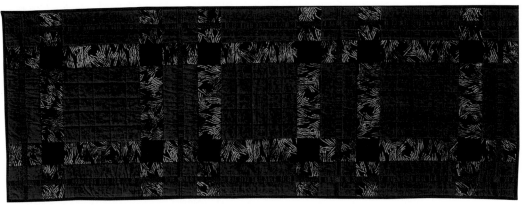

Elliot table runner, 25½″ × 67″ made by Kathy Allen, quilted by Shannon Ryan-Freeman, 2016

I chose these fabrics to reflect the traditional colors of the Elliot tartan. This table runner was my trial quilt: I wanted to see if the math worked and what the resulting quilt would look like. It can be said that I wrote this book because I liked this quilt!

Elliot square lap quilt, 67″ × 67″, made by Kathy Allen, quilted by Shannon Ryan-Freeman, 2016

This quilt is made entirely with hand-dyed fabric by Cherrywood Hand Dyed Fabrics, which has a distinctive suede look. The large spaces lend themselves to complex quilting designs that stand out, such as the Celtic designs quilted in the 10″ spaces.

Westminster Hall is the finest example of medieval architecture in Europe. Early in the morning on May 11, 1941, the chamber used for the House of Commons was set on fire by bombs and incendiaries (it was World War II). Colonel Walter Elliot, Member of Parliament, was busy fighting a fire on a neighboring street when he looked up and saw that the roof of Westminster Hall was on fire. He hurried to the spot and arranged with the chief superintendent to have all the water pumps in the area used to save Westminster Hall. He later went on to become Scotland's secretary of state. (On a side note, I'm not sure modern politicians would be so hands-on when it comes to fighting a fire as was Lord Elliot!)

The Elliot tartan has a base of true blue with large black stripes and thin maroon stripes that intersect. In some versions, there is no black and both the larger and smaller stripes are maroon. In this loose interpretation, I used black.

Not many of the Scottish tartans have a blue background (although there are many with blue stripes). MacLeod of Harris and McCorquodale have blue backgrounds. Campbell of Argyll's background is pale blue, but it's not at all like the true blue of Elliot.

TIP Fabric Selection

Fabrics A, D, and E will create a pattern that will be enhanced if these three fabrics are related and have a bit of a zing to them. In the pattern diagram shown here, A is pure red, D is red/black merge, and E is red/blue merge. The combination makes a red strip run through the dominant blue, creating the pattern. It also helps if these three fabrics are a lighter value than fabrics B, C, and F.

2″	¾″	2″	3″	10″	3″	2″	¾″	2″	
B	E	B	F	B	F	B	E	B	2″
E	A	E	D	E	D	E	A	E	¾″
B	E	B	F	B	F	B	E	B	2″
F	D	F	C	F	C	F	D	F	3″
B	E	B	F	B	F	B	E	B	10″
F	D	F	C	F	C	F	D	F	3″
B	E	B	F	B	F	B	E	B	2″
E	A	E	D	E	D	E	A	E	¾″
B	E	B	F	B	F	B	E	B	2″

A single woven pattern in my interpretation of the Elliot tartan. The *Elliot* quilts are created by repeating this pattern. The blue background (fabric B) is intersected by base colors black (fabric C) and red (fabric A), creating merge fabrics (D, E, and F).

Materials

Yardages are listed for the table runner /
square lap quilt / king quilt.

Red (A): ⅛ yard / ⅛ yard / ⅛ yard

Blue (B): 1¼ yards / 2¾ yards / 6 yards

Black (C): ⅓ yard / ⅝ yard / 1⅛ yards

Red/black merge (D): ⅓ yard / ½ yard / ¾ yard

Red/blue merge (E): ½ yard / 1⅛ yards / 1⅝ yards

Blue/black merge (F): ⅞ yard / 2⅜ yards / 5 yards

Backing: 2⅛ yards / 4¼ yards / 9¾ yards

Binding: ½ yard / ¾ yard / 1 yard

Cutting

Cut all strips across the width of fabric. These
strips will be used to create quadruple-strip
sets, triple-strip sets, and connectors. See How
to Build a Tartan Design (page 16) for detailed
instructions. Put a swatch of each fabric on
the fabric organization worksheet (page 110)
to help you keep your fabrics in order.

FABRIC		STRIP WIDTH	NUMBER OF STRIPS		
			Table runner	Square lap quilt	King quilt
Red (A)		1¼"	1	1	2
Blue (B)		10½"	1	4	10
		2½"	9	18	38
Black (C)		3½"	2	5	10
Red/black merge (D)		3½"	1	3	4
		1¼"	2	3	6
Red/blue merge (E)		10½"	0	1	1
		2½"	2	2	4
		1¼"	5	9	19
Blue/black merge (F)		10½"	0	1	2
		3½"	5	14	33
		2½"	4	6	12
Binding		2½"	6	8	12

Making the Quilt

Triplets, Quartets, and Connectors

Refer to the following lists to make strip sets from three fabrics for triple-strip sets or four fabrics for quadruple-strip sets. From the strip sets, subcut triplets and quartets.

Quartets

QUADRUPLE-STRIP SET 1 --

Make 3 strip sets for the table runner, 6 for the square lap quilt, or 13 for the king quilt. Subcut quartets 1 and 4.

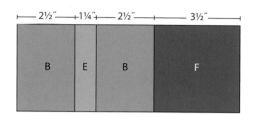

Table runner

⌐Quartet 4: 6 segments 10½″ wide

└Quartet 1: 16 segments 2½″ wide

Square lap quilt

⌐Quartet 4: 12 segments 10½″ wide

└Quartet 1: 32 segments 2½″ wide

King quilt

⌐Quartet 4: 30 segments 10½″ wide

└Quartet 1: 72 segments 2½″ wide

QUADRUPLE-STRIP SET 2 --

Make 1 strip set for the table runner or the square lap quilt or 2 strip sets for the king quilt. Subcut quartet 2.

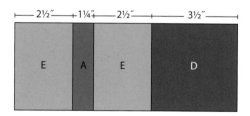

Table runner

—Quartet 2: 8 segments 1¼″ wide

Square lap quilt

—Quartet 2: 16 segments 1¼″ wide

King quilt

—Quartet 2: 36 segments 1¼″ wide

QUADRUPLE-STRIP SET 3 --

Make 2 strip sets for the table runner, 3 for the square lap quilt, or 6 for the king quilt. Subcut quartet 3.

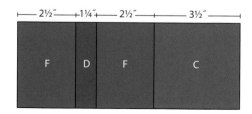

Table runner

—Quartet 3: 12 segments 3½″ wide

Square lap quilt

—Quartet 3: 24 segments 3½″ wide

King quilt

—Quartet 3: 60 segments 3½″ wide

Triplets

TRIPLE-STRIP SET 1 -

Make 2 strip sets for the square lap quilt or 5 for the king quilt (none for the table runner). Subcut triplets 1 and 4.

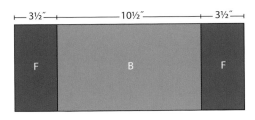

| ⊢ 3½″ ⊣ | ⊢ 10½″ ⊣ | ⊢ 3½″ ⊣ |

Square lap quilt

⌐ Triplet 4: 3 segments 10½″ wide

└ Triplet 1: 8 segments 2½″ wide

King quilt

⌐ Triplet 4: 10 segments 10½″ wide

└ Triplet 1: 24 segments 2½″ wide

TRIPLE-STRIP SET 2 -

Make 1 strip set for the square lap quilt or the king quilt (none for the table runner). Subcut triplet 2.

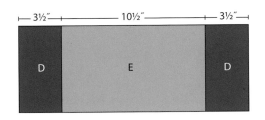

| ⊢ 3½″ ⊣ | ⊢ 10½″ ⊣ | ⊢ 3½″ ⊣ |

Square lap quilt

— Triplet 2: 4 segments 1¼″ wide

King quilt

— Triplet 2: 12 segments 1¼″ wide

TRIPLE-STRIP SET 3 -

Make 1 strip set for the square lap quilt or 2 for the king quilt (none for the table runner). Subcut triplet 3.

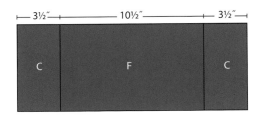

| ⊢ 3½″ ⊣ | ⊢ 10½″ ⊣ | ⊢ 3½″ ⊣ |

Square lap quilt

— Triplet 3: 6 segments 3½″ wide

King quilt

— Triplet 3: 20 segments 3½″ wide

Connectors

Subcut connectors from the strips left over after you have made the strip sets.

FABRIC		CONNECTOR NUMBER	STRIP WIDTH	SUBCUT SEGMENTS THIS WIDE	QUANTITY		
					Table runner	Square lap quilt	King quilt
Blue (B)		4	10½″	10½″	3	6	15
		1	2½″	10½″	8	16	36
Red/blue merge (E)		2	1¼″	10½″	4	8	18
Blue/black merge (F)		3	3½″	10½″	6	12	30

Quilt assembly for all three sizes -

King quilt

| Triplet | Quartet | Connector | Inverse Quartet | Row Type |

Making the Rows

Referring to the Row Types table for your quilt size (below and page 32), sew the triplets, quartets, and connectors together to make each type of row. To sew each row together, start with the piece listed at the left and add each segment in order from left to right. The numbers in each column refer to the quartet or connector number you made in Triplets, Quartets, and Connectors (page 28). Refer to How to Build a Tartan Design, Step 5 (page 20) for detailed instructions on how to assemble the rows.

Row Types—Table Runner

ROW TYPE AND NUMBER TO MAKE	QUARTET	CONNECTOR	INVERSE QUARTET
A: Make 8.	1	1	1
B: Make 4.	2	2	2
C: Make 6.	3	3	3
D: Make 3.	4	4	4

NOTE: Shorter Table Runner

For a shorter two-pattern table runner, repeat rows 1–6 only once, and then continue with the last three rows.

Row Types—Square Lap Quilt

ROW TYPE AND NUMBER TO MAKE	QUARTET	CONNECTOR	INVERSE QUARTET	TRIPLET	QUARTET	CONNECTOR	INVERSE QUARTET
A: Make 8.	1	1	1	1	1	1	1
B: Make 4.	2	2	2	2	2	2	2
C: Make 6.	3	3	3	3	3	3	3
D: Make 3.	4	4	4	4	4	4	4

Row Types—King Quilt

ROW TYPE AND NUMBER TO MAKE	QUARTET	CONNECTOR	INVERSE QUARTET	TRIPLET	QUARTET	CONNECTOR	INVERSE QUARTET	TRIPLET	QUARTET	CONNECTOR	INVERSE QUARTET
A: Make 12.	1	1	1	1	1	1	1	1	1	1	1
B: Make 6.	2	2	2	2	2	2	2	2	2	2	2
C: Make 10.	3	3	3	3	3	3	3	3	3	3	3
D: Make 5.	4	4	4	4	4	4	4	4	4	4	4

Quilt Assembly

Referring to the quilt assembly diagram (pages 30 and 31), sew the row types together in the indicated order to complete the quilt top. Press the seam allowances of each row in the opposite direction from adjacent rows. Pin at each and every seam intersection.

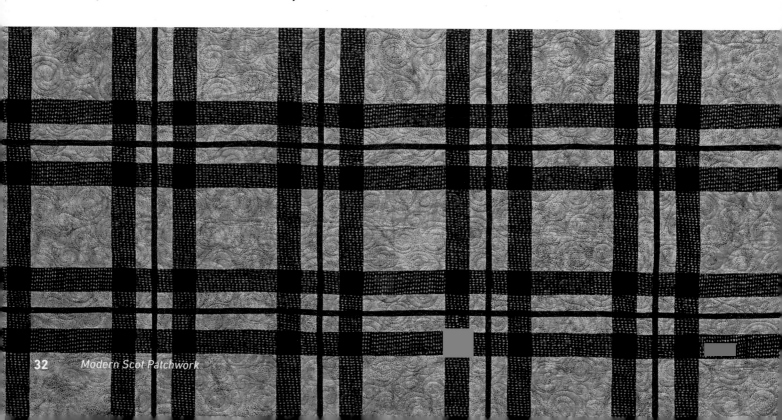

Skill Level:
BEGINNER

Maxwell

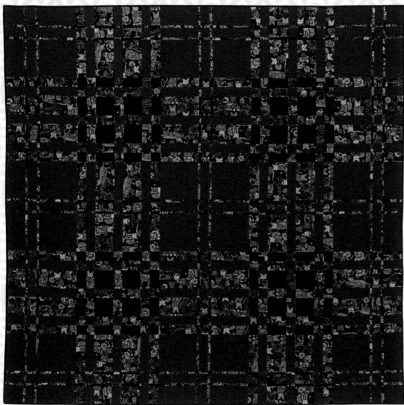

Maxwell sport lap quilt, 48″ × 48″, made by Kathy Allen, quilted by Shannon Ryan-Freeman, 2016.

Light Tomato by Clothworks and a solid black from Michael Miller Fabrics are complemented by the black-and-red merge fabric, Vibe by Ro Gregg for Paintbrush Studio Collections (Fabri-Quilt, Inc.). The 48″ × 48″ size is perfect for taking to sporting events.

Maxwell square full quilt, 85″ × 85″, made by Kathy Allen, quilted by Shannon Ryan-Freeman, 2016.

The whimsical cat fabric, which serves as the red/black merge, is an example of when the merge rules are ignored (page 11). Although the cat fabric is directional, it did not interfere with the overall design.

The most interesting of the Maxwells was the fifth Earl of Nithsdale, who was sentenced to death in Westminster Hall for the role he played in the 1715 Jacobite rebellion. He was gallantly rescued by his devoted wife on the night before he was to be executed. She repeatedly entered in and out of his prison cell with her attendants until the guards were confused as to who was in the cell and who was not. Secretly, the Earl had sneaked out of his prison cell disguised as one of his wife's attendants while his wife stayed behind. Later she left the prison cell with loud farewells to the empty room. The two lived the rest of their lives happily in poverty at the Chevalier's court in Rome until the earl died in 1744.

The Maxwell tartan is created by weaving just two colors together: dominant red for the background and black, which is often a dark green. Along with black, the merge fabric creates the pattern against the background. Consider the value against the background when selecting the merge fabric. This simple color combination is also seen in the Menzies hunting tartan, as well as the Moncrieffe and Erskine tartans.

4″	½″	2″	½″	8″	2″	2″	4″	2″	4″	2″	2″	8″	½″	2″	½″	4″	
A	C	A	C	A	C	A	C	A	C	A	C	A	C	A	C	A	4″
C	B	C	B	C	B	C	B	C	B	C	B	C	B	C	B	C	½″
A	C	A	C	A	C	A	C	A	C	A	C	A	C	A	C	A	2″
C	B	C	B	C	B	C	B	C	B	C	B	C	B	C	B	C	½″
A	C	A	C	A	C	A	C	A	C	A	C	A	C	A	C	A	8″
C	B	C	B	C	B	C	B	C	B	C	B	C	B	C	B	C	2″
A	C	A	C	A	C	A	C	A	C	A	C	A	C	A	C	A	2″
C	B	C	B	C	B	C	B	C	B	C	B	C	B	C	B	C	4″
A	C	A	C	A	C	A	C	A	C	A	C	A	C	A	C	A	2″
C	B	C	B	C	B	C	B	C	B	C	B	C	B	C	B	C	4″
A	C	A	C	A	C	A	C	A	C	A	C	A	C	A	C	A	2″
C	B	C	B	C	B	C	B	C	B	C	B	C	B	C	B	C	2″
A	C	A	C	A	C	A	C	A	C	A	C	A	C	A	C	A	8″
C	B	C	B	C	B	C	B	C	B	C	B	C	B	C	B	C	½″
A	C	A	C	A	C	A	C	A	C	A	C	A	C	A	C	A	2″
C	B	C	B	C	B	C	B	C	B	C	B	C	B	C	B	C	½″
A	C	A	C	A	C	A	C	A	C	A	C	A	C	A	C	A	4″

A single woven pattern in my interpretation of the Maxwell tartan. I've made this one-pattern diagram for the Maxwell tartan into a small square lap quilt, the perfect size to take to a sporting event. The other *Maxwell* quilt is created by repeating this pattern. The red background (fabric A) is intersected by three sizes of black (fabric B) stripes. Where the black fabric meets the red background, a red/black merge (fabric C) results.

Materials

Yardages are listed for the
sport lap quilt / square full quilt.

Red (A): 1½ yards / 3¾ yards

Black (B): ⅜ yard / 1¼ yards

Red/black merge (C): 1¼ yards / 3¾ yards

Backing: 3⅛ yards / 8 yards

Binding: ½ yard / 1 yard

Cutting

Cut all strips across the width of fabric. These
strips will be used to create quadruple-strip
sets, triple-strip sets, and connectors. See How
to Build a Tartan Design (page 16) for detailed
instructions. Put a swatch of each fabric on
the fabric organization worksheet (page 110) to
help you keep your fabrics in order.

FABRIC		STRIP WIDTH	NUMBER OF STRIPS	
			Sport lap quilt	Square full quilt
Red (A)		8½″	1	4
		4½″	3	6
		2½″	7	24
Black (B)		4½″	1	4
		2½″	1	4
		1″	2	6
Red/black merge (C)		4½″	4	13
		2½″	5	18
		1″	6	18
Binding		2½″	6	10

Making the Quilt

Triplets, Quartets, and Connectors

Refer to the following lists to make strip sets from three fabrics for triple-strip sets or four fabrics for quadruple-strip sets. From the strip sets, subcut triplets and quartets.

Quartets

QUADRUPLE-STRIP SET 1 -

Make 2 strip sets for the sport lap quilt or 4 for the square full quilt. Subcut quartets 1, 3, and 4.

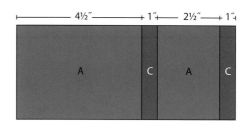

Sport lap quilt

- Quartet 4: 4 segments 8½″ wide
- Quartet 1: 4 segments 4½″ wide
- Quartet 3: 10 segments 2½″ wide

Square full quilt

- Quartet 4: 8 segments 8½″ wide
- Quartet 1: 4 segments 4½″ wide
- Quartet 3: 18 segments 2½″ wide

QUADRUPLE-STRIP SET 2 -

Make 1 strip set for the sport lap quilt or 2 for the square full quilt. Subcut quartets 2, 5, and 6.

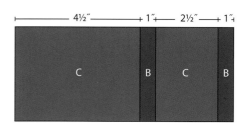

Sport lap quilt

- Quartet 6: 4 segments 4½″ wide
- Quartet 5: 4 segments 2½″ wide
- Quartet 2: 8 segments 1″ wide

Square full quilt

- Quartet 6: 8 segments 4½″ wide
- Quartet 5: 8 segments 2½″ wide
- Quartet 2: 12 segments 1″ wide

Triplets

TRIPLE-STRIP SET 1 --

Make 2 strip sets for the sport lap quilt or 7 for the square full quilt. Subcut triplets 1, 3, and 4.

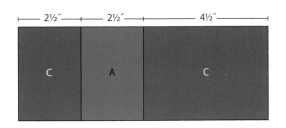

Sport lap quilt

- Triplet 4: 4 segments 8½" wide
- Triplet 1: 4 segments 4½" wide
- Triplet 3: 10 segments 2½" wide

Square full quilt

- Triplet 4: 16 segments 8½" wide
- Triplet 1: 8 segments 4½" wide
- Triplet 3: 36 segments 2½" wide

TRIPLE-STRIP SET 2 --

Make 1 strip set for the sport lap quilt or 4 for the square full quilt. Subcut triplets 2, 5, and 6.

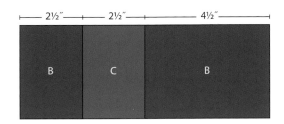

Sport lap quilt

- Triplet 6: 4 segments 4½" wide
- Triplet 5: 4 segments 2½" wide
- Triplet 2: 8 segments 1" wide

Square full quilt

- Triplet 6: 16 segments 4½" wide
- Triplet 5: 16 segments 2½" wide
- Triplet 2: 24 segments 1" wide

TRIPLE-STRIP SET 3 --

Make 2 strip sets for the square full quilt (none for the sport lap quilt). Subcut triplets 7, 9, and 10.

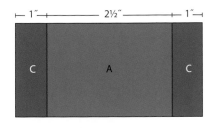

Square full quilt

- Triplet 10: 4 segments 8½" wide
- Triplet 7: 2 segments 4½" wide
- Triplet 9: 9 segments 2½" wide

TRIPLE-STRIP SET 4 --

Make 1 strip set for the square full quilt (none for the sport lap quilt). Subcut triplets 8, 11, and 12.

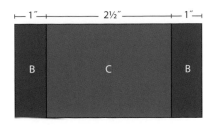

Square full quilt

- Triplet 12: 4 segments 4½" wide
- Triplet 11: 4 segments 2½" wide
- Triplet 8: 6 segments 1" wide

Connectors

Subcut connectors from the strips leftover after you have made the strip sets.

FABRIC		CONNECTOR NUMBER	STRIP WIDTH	SUBCUT SEGMENTS THIS WIDE	QUANTITY	
					Sport lap quilt	Square full quilt
Red (A)		7	8½"	8½"	4	16
		1	4½"	8½"	4	8
		2	4½"	2½"	2	4
		5	2½"	8½"	12	44
		6	2½"	2½"	5	18
Red/black merge (C)		10	4½"	8½"	4	16
		11	4½"	2½"	2	8
		8	2½"	8½"	4	16
		9	2½"	2½"	2	8
		3	1"	8½"	8	24
		4	1"	2½"	4	12

Making the Rows

Referring to the Row Types table for your quilt size (below and next page), sew the triplets, quartets, and connectors together to make each type of row. To sew each row together, start with the piece listed at the left and add each segment in order from left to right. The numbers in each column refer to the quartet or connector number you made in Triplets, Quartets, and Connectors (page 36). Refer to How to Build a Tartan Design, Step 5 (page 20) for detailed instructions on how to assemble the rows.

Row Types—Sport Lap Quilt

ROW TYPE AND NUMBER TO MAKE	QUARTET	CONNECTOR	TRIPLET	CONNECTOR	INVERSE TRIPLET	CONNECTOR	INVERSE QUARTET
A: Make 2.	1	1	1	2	1	1	1
B: Make 4.	2	3	2	4	2	3	2
C: Make 5.	3	5	3	6	3	5	3
D: Make 2.	4	7	4	5	4	7	4
E: Make 2.	5	8	5	9	5	8	5
F: Make 2.	6	10	6	11	6	10	6

Row Types—Square Full Quilt

ROW TYPE AND NUMBER TO MAKE	QUARTET	CONNECTOR	TRIPLET	CONNECTOR	INVERSE TRIPLET	CONNECTOR	TRIPLET	CONNECTOR	TRIPLET	CONNECTOR	INVERSE TRIPLET	CONNECTOR	INVERSE QUARTET
A: Make 2.	1	1	1	2	1	1	7	1	1	2	1	1	1
B: Make 6.	2	3	2	4	2	3	8	3	2	4	2	3	2
C: Make 9.	3	5	3	6	3	5	9	5	3	6	3	5	3
D: Make 4.	4	7	4	5	4	7	10	7	4	5	4	7	4
E: Make 4.	5	8	5	9	5	8	11	8	5	9	5	8	5
F: Make 4.	6	10	6	11	6	10	12	10	6	11	6	10	6

Quilt Assembly

Referring to the quilt assembly diagrams (at right and pages 40 and 41), sew the row types together in the indicated order to complete the quilt top. Press the seam allowances of each row in the opposite direction from adjacent rows. Pin at each and every seam intersection.

Sport lap quilt assembly

* Connector

Row number	Quartet	Connector	Triplet	*	Inverse Triplet	Connector	Triplet
1	1	1	1	2	1	1	7
2	2	3	2	4	2	3	8
3	3	5	3	6	3	5	9
4	2	3	2	4	2	3	8
5	4	7	4	5	4	7	10
6	5	8	5	9	5	8	11
7	3	5	3	6	3	5	9
8	6	10	6	11	6	10	12
9	3	5	3	6	3	5	9
10	6	10	6	11	6	10	12
11	3	5	3	6	3	5	9
12	5	8	5	9	5	8	11
13	4	7	4	5	4	7	10
14	2	3	2	4	2	3	8
15	3	5	3	6	3	5	9
16	2	3	2	4	2	3	8
17	4	7	4	5	4	7	10
18	5	8	5	9	5	8	11
19	3	5	3	6	3	5	9
20	6	10	6	11	6	10	12
21	3	5	3	6	3	5	9
22	6	10	6	11	6	10	12
23	3	5	3	6	3	5	9
24	5	8	5	9	5	8	11
25	4	7	4	5	4	7	10
26	2	3	2	4	2	3	8
27	3	5	3	6	3	5	9
28	2	3	2	4	2	3	8
29	1	1	1	2	1	1	7

Square full quilt assembly --

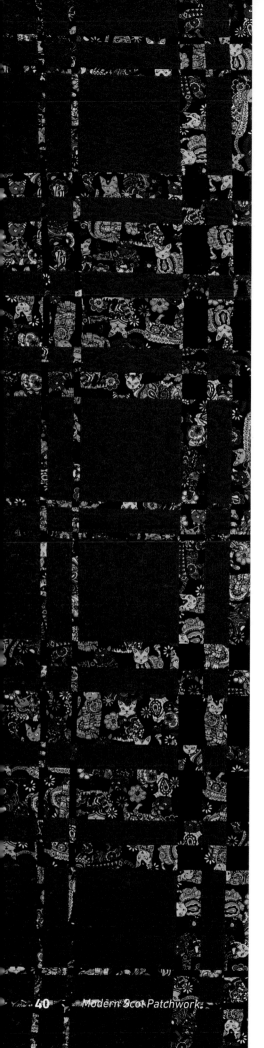

Connector	Triplet	*	Inverse Triplet	Connector	Inverse Quartet	Row type
1	1	2	1	1	1	A
3	2	4	2	3	2	B
5	3	6	3	5	3	C
3	2	4	2	3	2	B
7	4	5	4	7	4	D
8	5	9	5	8	5	E
5	3	6	3	5	3	C
10	6	11	6	10	6	F
5	3	6	3	5	3	C
10	6	11	6	10	6	F
5	3	6	3	5	3	C
8	5	9	5	8	5	E
7	4	5	4	7	4	D
3	2	4	2	3	2	B
5	3	6	3	5	3	C
3	2	4	2	3	2	B
7	4	5	4	7	4	D
8	5	9	5	8	5	E
5	3	6	3	5	3	C
10	6	11	6	10	6	F
5	3	6	3	5	3	C
10	6	11	6	10	6	F
5	3	6	3	5	3	C
8	5	9	5	8	5	E
7	4	5	4	7	4	D
3	2	4	2	3	2	B
5	3	6	3	5	3	C
3	2	4	2	3	2	B
1	1	2	1	1	1	A

* Connector

Skill Level:
EXPERIENCED

Maitland

Maitland square lap quilt, 57½″ × 57½″, made by Kathy Allen, quilted by Shannon Ryan-Freeman, 2016

The three sub-patterns of this square lap quilt, made with fabric in the traditional colors, are easily distinguishable against the olive green background. The tiny stripes of the outer color ring give the Maitland tartan its distinctive look.

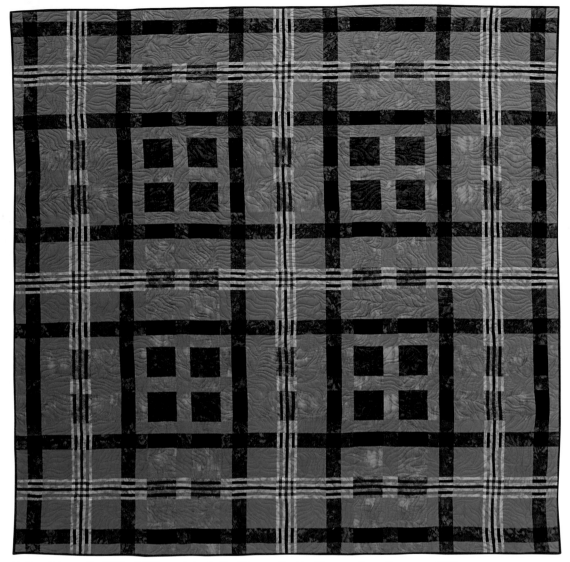

Maitland king quilt, 92½″ × 92½″, made by Kathy Allen, quilted by Shannon Ryan-Freeman, 2016

There are three sub-patterns against a Christmas-green background in this version, but the subtlety of the blue/green merge makes the largest of the sub-patterns almost disappear into the background, with the blue blocks seeming to appear from nowhere. Although, it is doubtful that anything would be noticed in this quilt other than the thin, bright color ring which gives the Maitland tartan its distinctive look.

The Maitlands are a lowland Scottish clan who originated in Normandy and traveled to Northumberland with William the Conqueror. The name, originally spelled *Mautalent*, means "foul-tempered" or "evil genius" in old French. (The men of those days wore their nicknames with pride!)

Thirlestane Castle is the historic seat of the chiefs (and later, earls) of Clan Maitland. During the Jacobite battle of 1745, Charles Stuart, who the Scots considered the rightful heir to the throne, stayed at Thirlestane Castle and had his army pitch their tents on the castle parklands. The Maitlands were considered neutral in the Jacobite wars, and so the English allowed them to keep their lands. A couple of hundred years later during World War II, Field Marshal Sir Henry Maitland Wilson commanded in the Middle East and succeeded U.S. General Dwight Eisenhower as supreme Allied commander.

The Maitland tartan, a beautiful pattern dominated by blue and green, has several tiny stripes that give the overall design a real pop. The Maitland tartan is actually a modification of the Lauder tartan, which is similar but doesn't have the thin yellow stripes.

In this loose interpretation of the Maitland tartan, the large, subtle stripes of blue against a green background are surrounded with dominant black stripes. The pattern will show best if the merge fabrics F and L are dark compared to the base fabrics A and E. The thin stripes give this quilt its dramatic effect (and why, along with having fifteen fabrics, its skill level is designated as experienced).

TIP Fabric Selection To make the thin stripes of the color ring stand out, I suggest that fabrics C, D, G, H, J, K, M, N, and O be tone-on-tone or a solid, and that fabrics C, D, G, and H be a lighter value than fabrics E, I, L, O, K, H, and M. Personally, I like to choose warm zinger fabrics for C, D, G, and H because they give the quilt a real pop against the cool colors of A, E, F, and L!

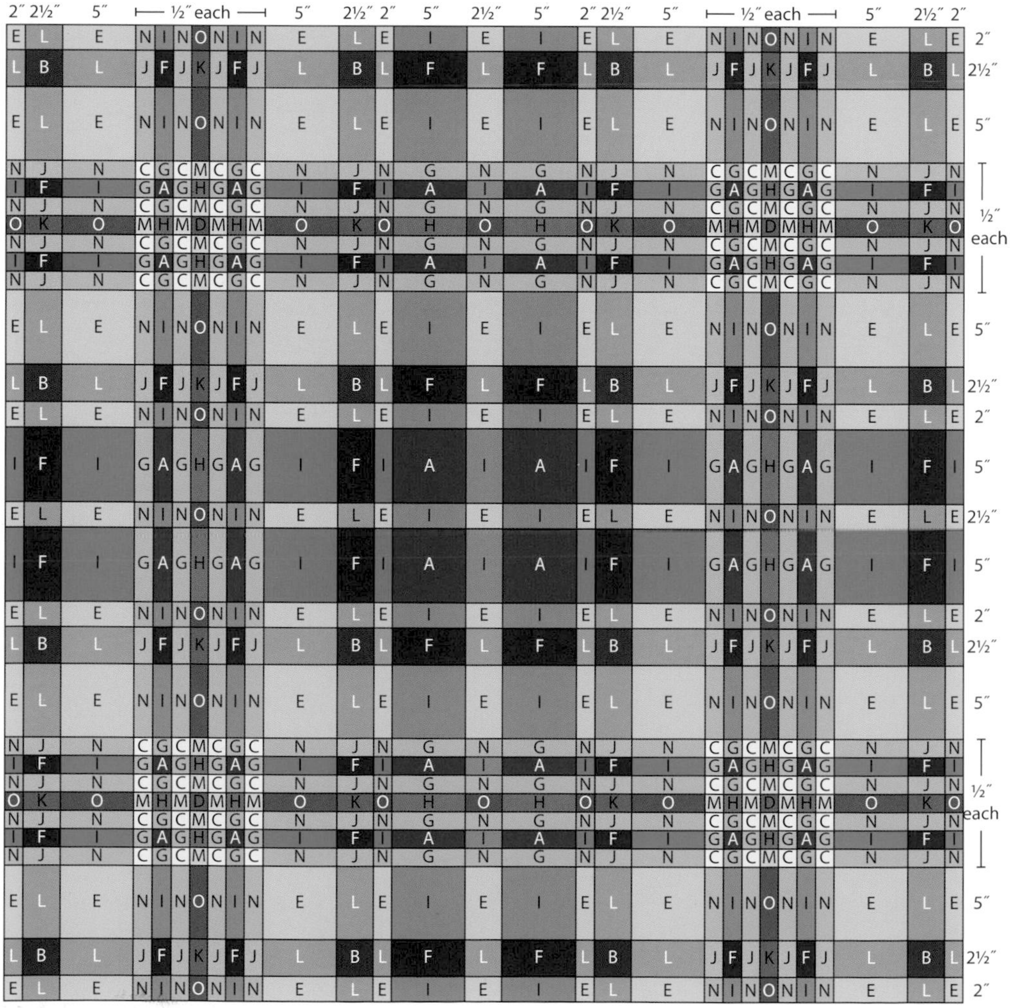

A single woven pattern in my interpretation of the Maitland tartan. The green background (fabric E) is intersected by base colors black (fabric B) and blue (fabric A), creating the two large patterns. The third pattern, a bright color ring, is created with base fabrics yellow (fabric C), blue (fabric A), and red (fabric D).

2"	2½"	5"	½"	½"	½"	½"	½"	½"	½"	5"	2½"	2"	5"	2½"	5"	2"	2½"	5"	½"	½"	½"	½"	½"	½"	½"	5"	2½"	2"	
E	L	E	N	I	N	O	N	I	N	E	L	E	I	E	I	E	L	E	N	I	N	O	N	I	N	E	L	E	2"
L	B	L	J	F	J	K	J	F	J	L	B	L	F	L	F	L	B	L	J	F	J	K	J	F	J	L	B	L	2½"
E	L	E	N	I	N	O	N	I	N	E	L	E	I	E	I	E	L	E	N	I	N	O	N	I	N	E	L	E	5"
N	J	N	C	G	C	M	C	G	C	N	J	N	G	N	G	N	J	N	C	G	C	M	C	G	C	N	J	N	½"
I	F	I	G	A	G	H	G	A	G	I	F	I	A	I	A	I	F	I	G	A	G	H	G	A	G	I	F	I	½"
N	J	N	C	G	C	M	C	G	C	N	J	N	G	N	G	N	J	N	C	G	C	M	C	G	C	N	J	N	½"
O	K	O	M	H	M	D	M	H	M	O	K	O	H	O	H	O	K	O	M	H	M	D	M	H	M	O	K	O	½"
N	J	N	C	G	C	M	C	G	C	N	J	N	G	N	G	N	J	N	C	G	C	M	C	G	C	N	J	N	½"
I	F	I	G	A	G	H	G	A	G	I	F	I	A	I	A	I	F	I	G	A	G	H	G	A	G	I	F	I	½"
N	J	N	C	G	C	M	C	G	C	N	J	N	G	N	G	N	J	N	C	G	C	M	C	G	C	N	J	N	½"
E	L	E	N	I	N	O	N	I	N	E	L	E	I	E	I	E	L	E	N	I	N	O	N	I	N	E	L	E	5"
L	B	L	J	F	J	K	J	F	J	L	B	L	F	L	F	L	B	L	J	F	J	K	J	F	J	L	B	L	2½"
E	L	E	N	I	N	O	N	I	N	E	L	E	I	E	I	E	L	E	N	I	N	O	N	I	N	E	L	E	2"
I	F	I	G	A	G	H	G	A	G	I	F	I	A	I	A	I	F	I	G	A	G	H	G	A	G	I	F	I	5"
E	L	E	N	I	N	O	N	I	N	E	L	E	I	E	I	E	L	E	N	I	N	O	N	I	N	E	L	E	2½"
I	F	I	G	A	G	H	G	A	G	I	F	I	A	I	A	I	F	I	G	A	G	H	G	A	G	I	F	I	5"
E	L	E	N	I	N	O	N	I	N	E	L	E	I	E	I	E	L	E	N	I	N	O	N	I	N	E	L	E	2"
L	B	L	J	F	J	K	J	F	J	L	B	L	F	L	F	L	B	L	J	F	J	K	J	F	J	L	B	L	2½"
E	L	E	N	I	N	O	N	I	N	E	L	E	I	E	I	E	L	E	N	I	N	O	N	I	N	E	L	E	5"
N	J	N	C	G	C	M	C	G	C	N	J	N	G	N	G	N	J	N	C	G	C	M	C	G	C	N	J	N	½"
I	F	I	G	A	G	H	G	A	G	I	F	I	A	I	A	I	F	I	G	A	G	H	G	A	G	I	F	I	½"
N	J	N	C	G	C	M	C	G	C	N	J	N	G	N	G	N	J	N	C	G	C	M	C	G	C	N	J	N	½"
O	K	O	M	H	M	D	M	H	M	O	K	O	H	O	H	O	K	O	M	H	M	D	M	H	M	O	K	O	½"
N	J	N	C	G	C	M	C	G	C	N	J	N	G	N	G	N	J	N	C	G	C	M	C	G	C	N	J	N	½"
I	F	I	G	A	G	H	G	A	G	I	F	I	A	I	A	I	F	I	G	A	G	H	G	A	G	I	F	I	½"
N	J	N	C	G	C	M	C	G	C	N	J	N	G	N	G	N	J	N	C	G	C	M	C	G	C	N	J	N	½"
E	L	E	N	I	N	O	N	I	N	E	L	E	I	E	I	E	L	E	N	I	N	O	N	I	N	E	L	E	5"
L	B	L	J	F	J	K	J	F	J	L	B	L	F	L	F	L	B	L	J	F	J	K	J	F	J	L	B	L	2½"
E	L	E	N	I	N	O	N	I	N	E	L	E	I	E	I	E	L	E	N	I	N	O	N	I	N	E	L	E	2"

Materials

Yardages are listed for the square
lap quilt / king quilt.

Blue (A): ⅝ yard / 1 yard

Black (B): ¼ yard / ⅜ yard

Yellow (C): ¼ yard / ¼ yard

Red (D): ⅛ yard / ⅛ yard

Green (E): 1¼ yards / 2½ yards

Blue/black merge (F): ¾ yard / 1 yard

Blue/yellow merge (G): ½ yard / ⅝ yard

Blue/red merge (H): ¼ yard / ⅜ yard

Blue/green merge (I): 1¼ yards / 2¾ yards

Black/yellow merge (J): ⅜ yard / ½ yard

Black/red merge (K): ⅛ yard / ¼ yard

Black/green merge (L): 1¼ yards / 1¾ yards

Yellow/red merge (M): ¼ yard / ¼ yard

Yellow/green merge (N): ⅝ yard / 1⅛ yards

Red/green merge (O): ⅛ yard / ⅜ yard

Backing: 3¾ yards / 8½ yards

Binding: ⅝ yard / 1 yard

Lauder tartan in ancient colors. The Lauder and Maitland clans—and their tartans—are closely related. The Maitland tartan is actually a modification of the Lauder tartan, which is similar but doesn't have the thin yellow stripes.

Cutting

Cut all strips across the width of fabric. These strips will be used to create triple-strip sets, seven-strip sets, and connectors. See How to Build a Tartan Design (page 16) for detailed instructions. Put a swatch of each fabric on the fabric organization worksheet (page 110) to help you keep your fabrics in order.

FABRIC		STRIP WIDTH	NUMBER OF STRIPS	
			Square lap quilt	King quilt
Blue (A)		5½"	2	4
		1"	4	8
Black (B)		3"	2	3
Yellow (C)		1"	4	4
Red (D)		1"	1	1
Green (E)		5½"	4	9
		3"	1	3
		2½"	4	9
Blue/black merge (F)		5½"	2	2
		3"	2	4
		1"	4	6
Blue/yellow merge (G)		1"	10	18
Blue/red merge (H)		1"	4	6
Blue/green merge (I)		5½"	4	10
		3"	1	2
		2½"	2	4
		1"	8	18
Black/yellow merge (J)		1"	8	12
Black/red merge (K)		1"	2	3
Black/green merge (L)		5½"	2	3
		3"	5	10
		2½"	2	3
Yellow/red merge (M)		1"	5	5
Yellow/green merge (N)		1"	16	36
Red/green merge (O)		1"	1	9
Binding		2½"	7	11

Making the Quilt

Triplets and Septets

Refer to the following lists to make strip sets from three fabrics for triple-strip sets or from seven fabrics for seven-strip sets. From the strip sets, subcut triplets and septets.

Maitland has a group of small strips, so instead of a triplet there is a septet, cut from a seven-strip set for the warp, and a "multi-row" for the weft. The multi-row is made by sewing the septets together side to side instead of end to end, and this should reduce the amount of distortion that is possible when using such thin rows. I like to make the two (square lap quilt) or three (king quilt) multi-rows first because they are the most time-consuming part of this quilt construction.

TIP ❖ **Stitch Length** Don't forget to make your stitches smaller, since these strip sets will be subcut into segments. This is especially important for the seven-strip sets!

Triplets

TRIPLE-STRIP SET 1	TRIPLE-STRIP SET 2	TRIPLE-STRIP SET 3
Make 4 strip sets for the square lap quilt or 9 for the king quilt. Subcut triplets 1, 3, and 5.	Make 2 strip sets for the square lap quilt or 3 for the king quilt. Subcut triplet 2.	Make 2 strip sets for the square lap quilt or 4 for the king quilt. Subcut triplet 4.

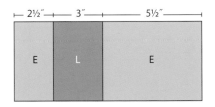

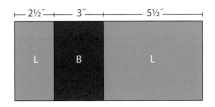

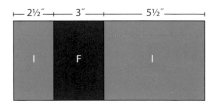

Square lap quilt

—Triplet 3: 16 segments 5½″ wide

—Triplet 5: 4 segments 3″ wide

—Triplet 1: 16 segments 2½″ wide

King quilt

—Triplet 3: 36 segments 5½″ wide

—Triplet 5: 12 segments 3″ wide

—Triplet 1: 36 segments 2½″ wide

Square lap quilt

—Triplet 2: 16 segments 3″ wide

King quilt

—Triplet 2: 36 segments 3″ wide

Square lap quilt

—Triplet 4: 8 segments 5½″ wide

King quilt

—Triplet 4: 24 segments 5½″ wide

TRIPLE-STRIP SET 4 -----------

Make 1 strip set for the square lap quilt or 3 for the king quilt. Subcut triplets 6, 8, and 10.

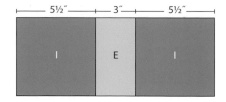

Square lap quilt

- **Triplet 8:** 4 segments 5½″ wide
- **Triplet 10:** 1 segment 3″ wide
- **Triplet 6:** 4 segments 2½″ wide

King quilt

- **Triplet 8:** 12 segments 5½″ wide
- **Triplet 10:** 4 segments 3″ wide
- **Triplet 6:** 12 segments 2½″ wide

TRIPLE-STRIP SET 5 -----------

Make 1 strip set for either quilt size. Subcut triplet 7.

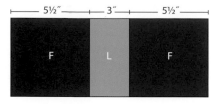

Square lap quilt

- **Triplet 7:** 4 segments 3″ wide

King quilt

- **Triplet 7:** 12 segments 3″ wide

TRIPLE-STRIP SET 6 -----------

Make 1 strip set for the square lap quilt or 2 for the king quilt. Subcut triplet 9.

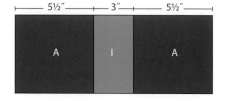

Square lap quilt

- **Triplet 9:** 2 segments 5½″ wide

King quilt

- **Triplet 9:** 8 segments 5½″ wide

Septets

Each strip that makes up the seven-strip sets is 1″, finishing to ½″. Create the seven-strip sets by first making 3 double-strip sets, sewing them together, and then adding the last strip.

SEVEN-STRIP SET 1 -----------

Make 4 strip sets for the square lap quilt or 9 for the king quilt. Subcut septets 1, 3, and 8.

Square lap quilt

- **Septet 3:** 16 segments 5½″ wide
- **Septet 8:** 4 segments 3″ wide
- **Septet 1:** 16 segments 2½″ wide

King quilt

- **Septet 3:** 36 segments 5½″ wide
- **Septet 8:** 12 segments 3″ wide
- **Septet 1:** 36 segments 2½″ wide

SEVEN-STRIP SET 2 -----------

Make 2 strip sets for the square lap quilt or 3 for the king quilt. Subcut septet 2.

Square lap quilt

- **Septet 2:** 16 segments 3″ wide

King quilt

- **Septet 2:** 36 segments 3″ wide

Make 1 strip set for either quilt size. Subcut septet 4.

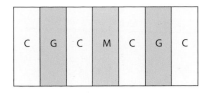

Square lap quilt

—**Septet 4:** 16 segments 1″ wide

King quilt

—**Septet 4:** 36 segments 1″ wide

Make 2 strip sets for the square lap quilt or 4 for the king quilt. Subcut septets 5 and 7.

Square lap quilt

┌**Septet 7:** 8 segments 5½″ wide

└**Septet 5:** 8 segments 1″ wide

King quilt

┌**Septet 7:** 24 segments 5½″ wide

└**Septet 5:** 18 segments 1″ wide

Make 1 strip set for either quilt size. Subcut septet 6.

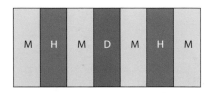

Square lap quilt

—**Septet 6:** 4 segments 1″ wide

King quilt

—**Septet 6:** 9 segments 1″ wide

Making the "Multi-Row"

Because the grouping of the thin strips might warp if sewn together as normal rows, you should sew these together first and then treat them as a single row, called a "multi-row." Being careful to pin at each seam junction, sew the following septets together *side to side* (not end to end) in the order indicated below. To make it easy to keep them in the proper order, I like to sew them together in groups.

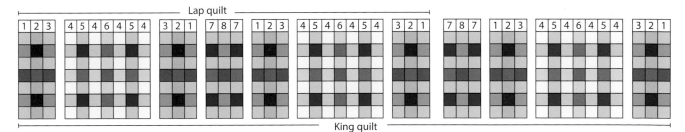

Sew the septets together side to side in the order indicated.

Making the Rows

Referring to the Row Types table for your quilt size (below), sew the triplets and septets together to make each type of row. To sew each row together, start with the piece listed at the left and add each segment in order from left to right. The numbers in each column refer to the triplet or septet number you made in Triplets and Septets (page 47). Refer to How to Build a Tartan Design, Step 5 (page 20) for detailed instructions on how to assemble the rows.

Row Types—Square Lap Quilt

ROW TYPE AND NUMBER TO MAKE	TRIPLET	SEPTET	INVERSE TRIPLET	TRIPLET	TRIPLET	SEPTET	INVERSE TRIPLET
A: Make 4.	1	1	1	6	1	1	1
B: Make 4.	2	2	2	7	2	2	2
C: Make 4.	3	3	3	8	3	3	3
D: Make 2.	Multi-row						
E: Make 2.	4	7	4	9	4	7	4
F: Make 1.	5	8	5	10	5	8	5

Row Types—King Quilt

ROW TYPE AND NUMBER TO MAKE	TRIPLET	SEPTET	INVERSE TRIPLET	TRIPLET	TRIPLET	SEPTET	INVERSE TRIPLET	TRIPLET	TRIPLET	SEPTET	INVERSE TRIPLET
A: Make 6.	1	1	1	6	1	1	1	6	1	1	1
B: Make 6.	2	2	2	7	2	2	2	7	2	2	2
C: Make 6.	3	3	3	8	3	3	3	8	3	3	3
D: Make 3.	Multi-row										
E: Make 4.	4	7	4	9	4	7	4	9	4	7	4
F: Make 2.	5	8	5	10	5	8	5	10	5	8	5

Quilt Assembly

Referring to the quilt assembly diagram, sew the row types together in the indicated order to complete the quilt top. Press the seam allowances of each row in the opposite direction from adjacent rows. Pin at each and every seam intersection.

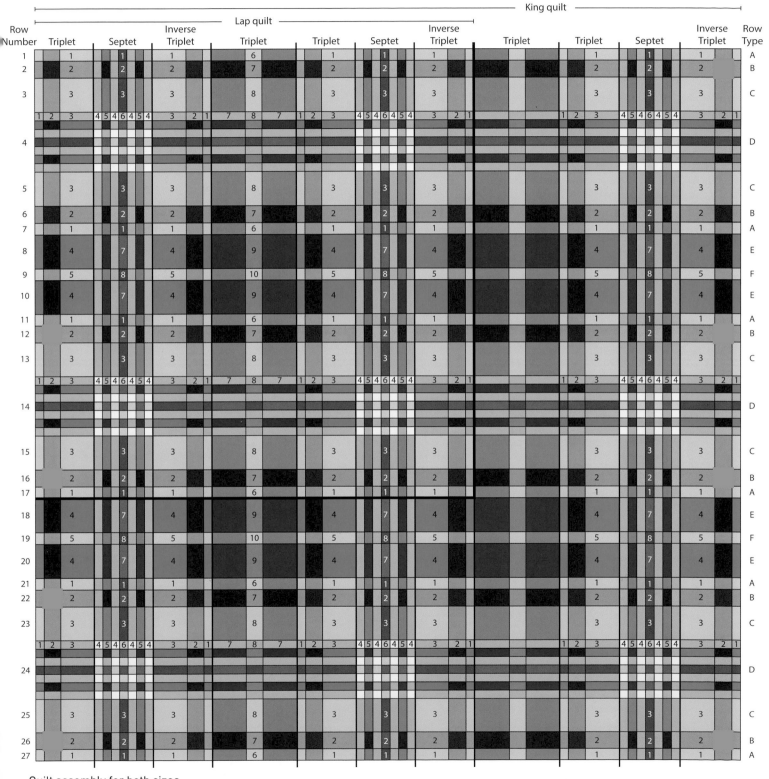

Quilt assembly for both sizes ---

Skill Level:
BEGINNER

Barclay

Barclay square full quilt, 81″ × 81″, made by Kathy Allen, quilted by Shannon Ryan-Freeman, 2016

Made entirely with Moda's Grunge fabric in traditional colors, this quilt provides a cheery splash of color to any room.

Barclay table runner, 28½″ × 63½″, made by Kathy Allen, quilted by Shannon Ryan-Freeman, 2016

The white base was replaced with green in this autumn-inspired table runner. The replacement of a single base can change the overall appearance of these tartan designs.

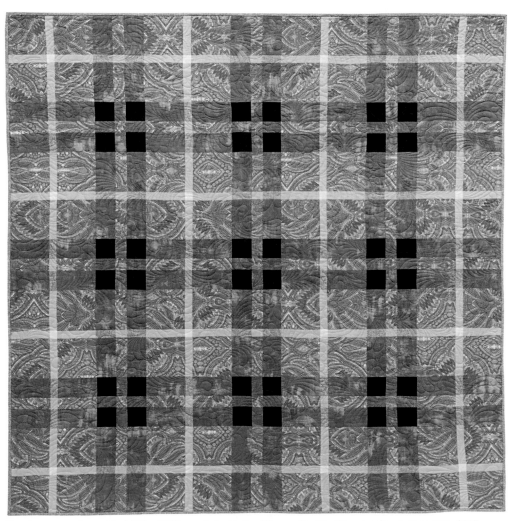

Barclay square lap quilt, 63½″ × 63½″, made by Kathy Allen, quilted by Shannon Ryan-Freeman, 2017

I had intended to use these fabrics for a tablecloth, but they called out to me that they wanted to be in this square lap quilt. Although the base colors were traditional yellow, black, and white, my yellow is dark with an intricate geometric pattern.

A quick note about Colonel Barclay of Urie: In 1648 he took up arms and served as the Scottish representative for Cromwell. He ended up in prison on suspicion of hostility to the new regime and shared a cell with the laird of Swinton, a Quaker, who converted Colonel Barclay to the beliefs of the Society of Friends. Barclay's son, Robert, embraced the Quaker beliefs of peace and love as well and became a most eloquent apologist, traveling with William Penn throughout Europe. Both men brought respect to the Quaker religion.

In contrast, the Barclays of Towie were more war-like. They produced Russian Field Marshal Michael Andreas, Prince Barclay de Tolly. He commanded the army that defeated Napoleon in 1812, three years before Wellington did the same thing at Waterloo.

The Barclay dress tartan is comprised of the three base colors of bright yellow, black, and thin stripes of white. It is very similar to the MacLeod of Lewis tartan, which is identical except that the thin stripes are red. In the Barclay hunting tartan, the yellow is replaced with forest green and the white with orange.

TIP Fabric Selection Consider value carefully when selecting the six fabrics for a traditional version of this project. There should be light and dark, and the six fabrics should be distinctive but fall within these two categories. To make the pattern stand out even more, make the background (fabric A) either darker or lighter than all the remaining fabrics.

A single woven pattern in my interpretation of the Barclay tartan. The Barclay quilts are created by repeating this pattern. The yellow background (fabric A) is intersected by base colors black (fabric B) and white (fabric C), creating black merge fabrics (E and F) and white merge fabrics (D and F).

5″	1″	5″	2½″	1½″	2½″	5″	1″	5″	
A	D	A	E	A	E	A	D	A	5″
D	C	D	F	D	F	D	C	D	1″
A	D	A	E	A	E	A	D	A	5″
E	F	E	B	F	B	E	F	E	2½″
A	D	A	F	A	F	A	D	A	1½″
E	F	E	B	F	B	E	F	E	2½″
A	D	A	E	A	E	A	D	A	5″
D	C	D	F	D	F	D	C	D	1″
A	D	A	E	A	E	A	D	A	5″

Materials

Yardages are listed for the table runner / square lap
quilt / square full quilt.

Yellow (A): 1¼ yards / 2⅛ yards / 3½ yards

Black (B): ⅜ yard / ½ yard / ⅝ yard

White (C): ⅛ yard / ⅛ yard / ⅛ yard

Yellow/white merge (D): ¾ yard / 1 yard / 1 yard

Yellow/black merge (E): 1 yard / 1¾ yards / 2¾ yards

Black/white merge (F): ⅜ yard / ⅜ yard / ½ yard

Backing: 2 yards / 4 yards / 6¾ yards

Binding: ½ yard / ⅝ yard / ¾ yard

Cutting

Cut all strips across the width of fabric. These
strips will be used to create triple-strip sets. See
How to Build a Tartan Design (page 16) for detailed
instructions. Put a swatch of each fabric on the
fabric organization worksheet (page 110) to help
you keep your fabrics in order.

FABRIC	STRIP WIDTH	NUMBER OF STRIPS		
		Table runner	Square lap quilt	Square full quilt
Yellow (A)	5½"	6	10	18
	2"	2	4	7
Black (B)	3"	2	4	6
White (C)	1½"	1	1	1
Yellow/white merge (D)	5½"	2	2	2
	2"	1	1	1
	1½"	3	5	9
Yellow/black merge (E)	5½"	2	4	6
	3"	4	8	14
	2"	1	2	3
Black/white merge (F)	3"	2	2	2
	1½"	1	2	3
Binding	2½"	6	7	9

Making the Quilt

Triplets, Triplets, and More Triplets!

Refer to the following lists to make strip sets from three fabrics for triple-strip sets. From the strip sets, subcut triplets.

TRIPLE-STRIP SET 1 --

Make 3 strip sets for the table runner, 5 for the square lap quilt, or 9 for the square full quilt. Subcut triplets 1 and 4.

Note: If the usable width of fabric is only 40″, an additional strip set may be needed for the square lap quilt.

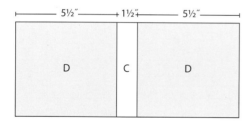

Table runner

⌐ Triplet 1: 16 segments 5½″ wide
⌐
└ Triplet 4: 6 segments 2″ wide

Square lap quilt

⌐ Triplet 1: 32 segments 5½″ wide
⌐
└ Triplet 4: 12 segments 2″ wide

Square full quilt

⌐ Triplet 1: 50 segments 5½″ wide
⌐
└ Triplet 4: 20 segments 2″ wide

TRIPLE-STRIP SET 2 --

Make 1 strip set for any project size. Subcut triplet 2.

Table runner

— Triplet 2: 8 segments 1½″ wide

Square lap quilt

— Triplet 2: 16 segments 1½″ wide

Square full quilt

— Triplet 2: 25 segments 1½″ wide

TRIPLE-STRIP SET 3 --

Make 1 strip set for the table runner, 2 for the square lap quilt, or 3 for the square full quilt. Subcut triplet 3.

Note: If the usable width of fabric is only 40″, an additional strip set may be needed for the square full quilt.

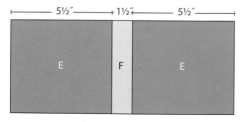

Table runner

— Triplet 3: 12 segments 3″ wide

Square lap quilt

— Triplet 3: 24 segments 3″ wide

Square full quilt

— Triplet 3: 40 segments 3″ wide

Make 2 strip sets for the table runner, 4 for the square lap quilt, or 7 for the square full quilt. Subcut triplets 5 and 8.

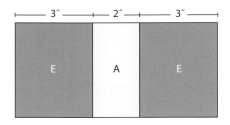

Table runner

⌐Triplet 5: 8 segments 5½″ wide

└Triplet 8: 3 segments 2″ wide

Square lap quilt

⌐Triplet 5: 24 segments 5½″ wide

└Triplet 8: 9 segments 2″ wide

Square full quilt

⌐Triplet 5: 40 segments 5½″ wide

└Triplet 8: 16 segments 2″ wide

Make 1 strip set for any project size. Subcut triplet 6.

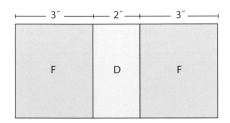

Table runner

—Triplet 6: 4 segments 1½″ wide

Square lap quilt

—Triplet 6: 12 segments 1½″ wide

Square full quilt

—Triplet 6: 20 segments 1½″ wide

Make 1 strip set for the table runner, 2 for the square lap quilt, or 3 for the square full quilt. Subcut triplet 7.

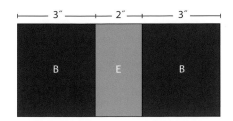

Table runner

—Triplet 7: 6 segments 3″ wide

Square lap quilt

—Triplet 7: 18 segments 3″ wide

Square full quilt

—Triplet 7: 32 segments 3″ wide

Making the Rows

Referring to the Row Types table for your quilt size (at right and below), sew the triplets together to make each type of row. To sew each row together, start with the piece listed at the left and add each segment in order from left to right. The numbers in each column refer to the triplet number you made in Triplets, Triplets, and More Triplets! (page 56). Refer to How to Build a Tartan Design, Step 5 (page 20) for detailed instructions on how to assemble the rows.

TIP **Palindromes** Both the segments and the rows of all *Barclay* projects are palindromes (reading the same forward and backward). When sewing the components together, press the seam allowances in the same direction. When assembling the quilt, place the rows so the seam allowances fall in alternate directions from row to row, making it easier to nest the seams as you pin and to make the corners neat and clean.

Row Types—Table Runner

ROW TYPE AND NUMBER TO MAKE	TRIPLET	TRIPLET	TRIPLET
A: Make 8.	1	5	1
B: Make 4.	2	6	2
C: Make 6.	3	7	3
D: Make 3.	4	8	4

NOTE: Shorter Table Runner

For a shorter two-pattern table runner than shown on the quilt assembly diagram (next page), repeat rows 1–6 only once, and then continue with the last three rows.

Row Types—Square Lap Quilt

ROW TYPE AND NUMBER TO MAKE	TRIPLET	TRIPLET	TRIPLET	TRIPLET	TRIPLET	TRIPLET	TRIPLET
A: Make 8.	1	5	1	5	1	5	1
B: Make 4.	2	6	2	6	2	6	2
C: Make 6.	3	7	3	7	3	7	3
D: Make 3.	4	8	4	8	4	8	4

Row Types—Square Full Quilt

ROW TYPE AND NUMBER TO MAKE	TRIPLET	TRIPLET	TRIPLET	TRIPLET	TRIPLET	TRIPLET	TRIPLET	TRIPLET	TRIPLET
A: Make 10.	1	5	1	5	1	5	1	5	1
B: Make 5.	2	6	2	6	2	6	2	6	2
C: Make 8.	3	7	3	7	3	7	3	7	3
D: Make 4.	4	8	4	8	4	8	4	8	4

Quilt Assembly

Referring to the quilt assembly diagram, sew the row types together in the indicated order to complete the quilt top. Press the seam allowances of each row in the opposite direction from adjacent rows. Pin at each and every seam intersection.

Row Number	Triplet	Triplet	Triplet	Triplet	Triplet	Triplet	Triplet	Triplet	Triplet	Row Type
1	1	5	1	5	1	5	1	5	1	A
2	2	6	2	6	2	6	2	6	2	B
3	1	5	1	5	1	5	1	5	1	A
4	3	7	3	7	3	7	3	7	3	C
5	4	8	4	8	4	8	4	8	4	D
6	3	7	3	7	3	7	3	7	3	C
7	1	5	1	5	1	5	1	5	1	A
8	2	6	2	6	2	6	2	6	2	B
9	1	5	1	5	1	5	1	5	1	A
10	3	7	3	7	3	7	3	7	3	C
11	4	8	4	8	4	8	4	8	4	D
12	3	7	3	7	3	7	3	7	3	C
13	1	5	1	5	1	5	1	5	1	A
14	2	6	2	6	2	6	2	6	2	B
15	1	5	1	5	1	5	1	5	1	A
16	3	7	3	7	3	7	3	7	3	C
17	4	8	4	8	4	8	4	8	4	D
18	3	7	3	7	3	7	3	7	3	C
19	1	5	1	5	1	5	1	5	1	A
20	2	6	2	6	2	6	2	6	2	B
21	1	5	1	5	1	5	1	5	1	A
22	3	7	3	7	3	7	3	7	3	C
23	4	8	4	8	4	8	4	8	4	D
24	3	7	3	7	3	7	3	7	3	C
25	1	5	1	5	1	5	1	5	1	A
26	2	6	2	6	2	6	2	6	2	B
27	1	5	1	5	1	5	1	5	1	A

Table runner · Lap quilt · Full quilt

Quilt assembly for all three sizes -

Skill Level:
EXPERIENCED

Hannay

Hannay square queen quilt, 95½″ × 95½″, made by Kathy Allen, quilted by Shannon Ryan-Freeman, 2016

The orange color ring intersects the white background and neutral strips. This color combination, along with the geometric quilting, give this quilt a masculine feel. This is my husband's favorite quilt of all time.

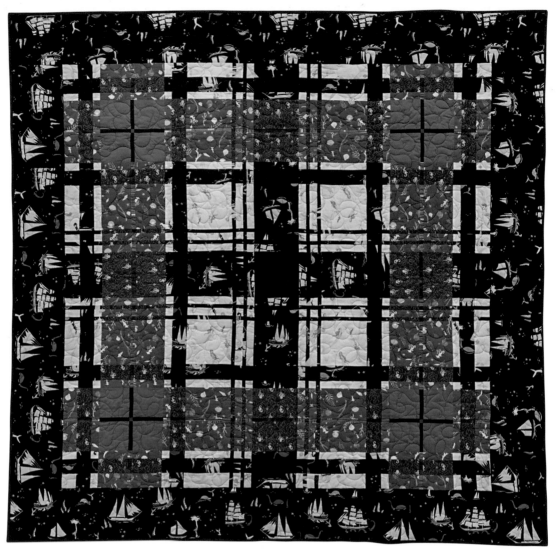

Hannay square lap quilt (with border), 71″ × 71″, made by Kathy Allen, quilted by Shannon Ryan-Freeman, 2016

The whimsical mermaids and ocean theme demonstrate that absolutely any fabric can be used to create interesting tartan quilts. This quilt is a good example of what happens when I wander away from my typical solids and tone-on-tones. Like the *Maxwell* cat quilt (page 33), the fabric print is directional; however, this did not interfere with the overall design. The fabrics are a mixture of the Saltwater collection by Emily Winfield Martin and the Mod Basics line, both organic lines from Birch Fabrics. I couldn't resist adding the border, which is optional in the pattern.

The Hannays were a lowland clan. The best known Hannay was James Hannay, the Dean of St. Giles' Cathedral in Edinburgh, which is the primary place of worship for those who belong to the Church of Scotland. In 1637, Charles I and Archbishop Laud intended to force the Anglican religion on all of Scotland. The *Book of Common Prayer* was revised, and James Hannay was required to use it instead of what had been used before. As he started to read the new liturgy, he heard an angry cry: "Thou false thief, dost thou say Mass at my lug?" It was Jenny Geddes, and as she yelled, she threw her stool at James's head. The incident began a full-scale riot that took the town guard to control. The disturbance led to the Bishops' Wars, which eventually led to the English Civil Wars. Interestingly, the eighteenth-century historian who recorded these events was William Maitland, whose tartan is also described in this book (page 42).

The *Hannay* has several tiny strips in its design, as does the *Maitland*. And so, like the *Maitland*, the *Hannay* has a multi-row in its design to prevent as much warping as possible of these tiny strips. I like to make the two (square lap quilt) or four (square queen quilt) multi-rows first. They are the most time-consuming part of this quilt. Although there are other ½" rows within the quilt, the multi-row section helps prevent distortion when several of these are together. When you have completed the multi-row, you can treat it as a single row.

The Hannay tartan has a white background with the pattern comprised of a ring of color. Focus colors are traditionally either orange with blue dissecting lines or purple with yellow dissecting lines. This project shows the combination of orange with blue dissecting lines.

TIP Fabric Selection For the most dramatic impact, ensure that the fabrics comprising the color ring (fabrics C–J) are different enough from fabrics A and B, which in my traditional sample are black and white. The color ring will stand out more if fabrics C, F, and G are in the same color family (in this case, orange). The same goes for the fabrics in the thin stripe that dissect the main color ring: fabrics D, I, and J (in this case, blue).

A single woven pattern in my interpretation of the Hannay tartan. The *Hannay* quilts are created by repeating this pattern. The white background (fabric A) is intersected by black (fabric B). A large orange color ring surrounds the pattern.

2"	2"	1"	4"	½"	4"	1"	2"	6"	½"	1"	½"	1"	6"	1"	½"	1"	½"	6"	2"	1"	4"	½"	4"	1"	2"	2"	
A	E	A	F	J	F	A	E	A	E	A	E	A	E	A	E	A	E	A	E	A	F	J	F	A	E	A	2"
E	B	E	G	I	G	E	B	E	B	E	B	E	B	E	B	E	B	E	B	E	G	I	G	E	B	E	2"
A	E	A	F	J	F	A	E	A	E	A	E	A	E	A	E	A	E	A	E	A	F	J	F	A	E	A	1"
F	G	F	C	H	C	F	G	F	G	F	G	F	G	F	G	F	G	F	G	F	C	H	C	F	G	F	4"
J	I	J	H	D	H	J	I	J	I	J	I	J	I	J	I	J	I	J	I	J	H	D	H	J	I	J	½"
F	G	F	C	H	C	F	G	F	G	F	G	F	G	F	G	F	G	F	G	F	C	H	C	F	G	F	4"
A	E	A	F	J	F	A	E	A	E	A	E	A	E	A	E	A	E	A	E	A	F	J	F	A	E	A	1"
E	B	E	G	I	G	E	B	E	B	E	B	E	B	E	B	E	B	E	B	E	G	I	G	E	B	E	2"
A	E	A	F	J	F	A	E	A	E	A	E	A	E	A	E	A	E	A	E	A	F	J	F	A	E	A	6"
E	B	E	G	I	G	E	B	E	B	E	B	E	B	E	B	E	B	E	B	E	G	I	G	E	B	E	½"
A	E	A	F	J	F	A	E	A	E	A	E	A	E	A	E	A	E	A	E	A	F	J	F	A	E	A	1"
E	B	E	G	I	G	E	B	E	B	E	B	E	B	E	B	E	B	E	B	E	G	I	G	E	B	E	½"
A	E	A	F	J	F	A	E	A	E	A	E	A	E	A	E	A	E	A	E	A	F	J	F	A	E	A	1"
E	B	E	G	I	G	E	B	E	B	E	B	E	B	E	B	E	B	E	B	E	G	I	G	E	B	E	6"
A	E	A	F	J	F	A	E	A	E	A	E	A	E	A	E	A	E	A	E	A	F	J	F	A	E	A	1"
E	B	E	G	I	G	E	B	E	B	E	B	E	B	E	B	E	B	E	B	E	G	I	G	E	B	E	½"
A	E	A	F	J	F	A	E	A	E	A	E	A	E	A	E	A	E	A	E	A	F	J	F	A	E	A	1"
E	B	E	G	I	G	E	B	E	B	E	B	E	B	E	B	E	B	E	B	E	G	I	G	E	B	E	½"
A	E	A	F	J	F	A	E	A	E	A	E	A	E	A	E	A	E	A	E	A	F	J	F	A	E	A	6"
E	B	E	G	I	G	E	B	E	B	E	B	E	B	E	B	E	B	E	B	E	G	I	G	E	B	E	2"
A	E	A	F	J	F	A	E	A	E	A	E	A	E	A	E	A	E	A	E	A	F	J	F	A	E	A	1"
F	G	F	C	H	C	F	G	F	G	F	G	F	G	F	G	F	G	F	G	F	C	H	C	F	G	F	4"
J	I	J	H	D	H	J	I	J	I	J	I	J	I	J	I	J	I	J	I	J	H	D	H	J	I	J	½"
F	G	F	C	H	C	F	G	F	G	F	G	F	G	F	G	F	G	F	G	F	C	H	C	F	G	F	4"
A	E	A	F	J	F	A	E	A	E	A	E	A	E	A	E	A	E	A	E	A	F	J	F	A	E	A	1"
E	B	E	G	I	G	E	B	E	B	E	B	E	B	E	B	E	B	E	B	E	G	I	G	E	B	E	2"
A	E	A	F	J	F	A	E	A	E	A	E	A	E	A	E	A	E	A	E	A	F	J	F	A	E	A	2"

Materials

Yardages are listed for the square lap quilt / square queen quilt.

White (A): 1⅛ yards / 2½ yards

Black (B): ⅝ yard / 1½ yards

Orange (C): ½ yard / 1 yard

Blue (D): ⅛ yard / ⅛ yard

White/black merge (E): 1½ yards / 3¼ yards

White/orange merge (F): 1¼ yards / 2¾ yards

Black/orange merge (G): 1 yard / 2 yards

Blue/orange merge (H): ½ yard / ½ yard

Blue/black merge (I): ⅝ yard / ⅝ yard

Blue/white merge (J): ⅝ yard / ¾ yard

Backing: 4½ yards / 8¾ yards

Binding: ¾ yard / 1 yard

Border for square lap quilt (*optional*): 1¾ yards

Cutting

Cut all strips across the width of fabric. These strips will be used to create quadruple-strip sets, triple-strip sets, and connectors. See How to Build a Tartan Design (page 16) for detailed instructions. Put a swatch of each fabric on the fabric organization worksheet (page 110) to help you keep your fabrics in order.

TIP **Labeling** The *Hannay* has 10 fabrics used to create 21 different triplets (from 12 different triple-strip sets). This is a lot to keep track of in addition to the 8 quartets and 7 connectors. Be sure to label your fabric and the triplets and quartets! It's easy to get them mixed up. I usually type numbers on a piece of paper, cut them up, and then pin the numbers on the stack of appropriate triplets and quartets—the same for the connectors.

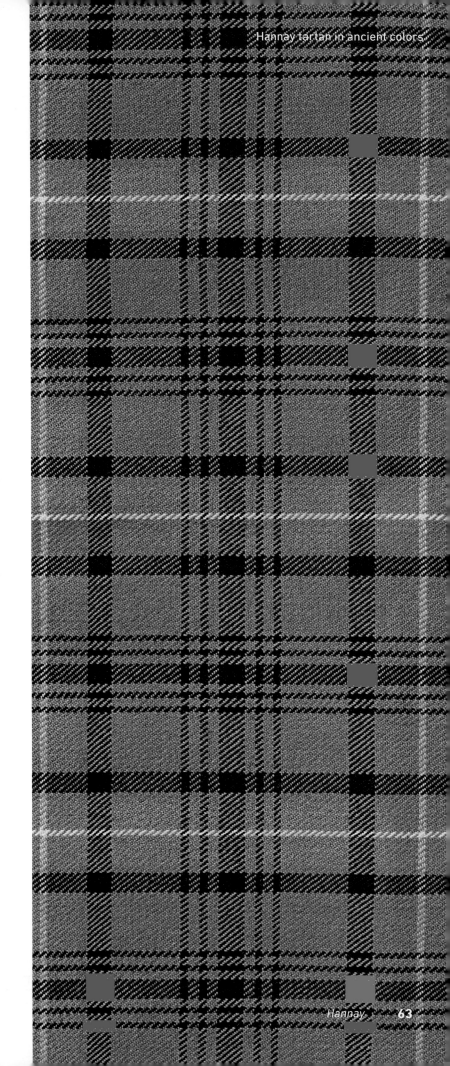

FABRIC		STRIP WIDTH	NUMBER OF STRIPS	
			Square lap quilt	Square queen quilt
White (A)		6½"	2	5
		2½"	2	2
		1½"	10	27
Black (B)		6½"*	1	2
		2½"	2	6
		1"	4	12
Orange (C)		4½"	2	6
Blue (D)		1"	1	1
White/black merge (E)		6½"	2	6
		2½"	5	10
		1½"	6	17
		1"	6	20
White/orange merge (F)		6½"	1	3
		4½"	4	6
		2½"	1	2
		1½"	6	17
Black/orange merge (G)		6½"	0	2
		4½"	3	6
		2½"	2	5
		1"	4	12
Blue/orange merge (H)		4½"	2	2
		1"	1	3
Blue/black merge (I)		6½"	0	1*
		2½"	2	2
		1"	4	5
Blue/white merge (J)		6½"	1	1
		2½"	1	1
		1½"	4	4
		1"	2	3
Binding		2½"	8	11
Border for square lap quilt (optional)		7¼"	7	0

* For connectors only

Making the Quilt

Triplets, Quartets, and Connectors

Refer to the following lists to make strip sets from three fabrics for triple-strip sets or four fabrics for quadruple-strip sets. From the strip sets, subcut triplets and quartets.

Triplets

TRIPLE-STRIP SET 1 - - - - - - - -

Make 2 strip sets for either quilt size. Subcut triplets 1, 3, and 6.

Note: If the usable width of fabric is only 40″, an additional strip set may be needed for the square queen quilt.

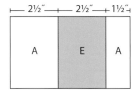

Square lap quilt

- Triplet 6: 4 segments 6½″ wide
- Triplet 1: 4 segments 2½″ wide
- Triplet 3: 8 segments 1½″ wide

Square queen quilt

- Triplet 6: 8 segments 6½″ wide
- Triplet 1: 4 segments 2½″ wide
- Triplet 3: 12 segments 1½″ wide

TRIPLE-STRIP SET 2 - - - - - - - -

Make 1 strip set for the square lap quilt or 3 for the square queen quilt. Subcut triplets 2 and 7.

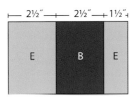

Square lap quilt

- Triplet 7: 2 segments 6½″ wide
- Triplet 2: 8 segments 2½″ wide

Square queen quilt

- Triplet 7: 8 segments 6½″ wide
- Triplet 2: 12 segments 2½″ wide

TRIPLE-STRIP SET 3 - - - - - - - -

Make 1 strip set for the square lap quilt or 2 for the square queen quilt. Subcut triplet 4.

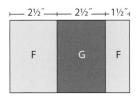

Square lap quilt

- Triplet 4: 8 segments 4½″ wide

Square queen quilt

- Triplet 4: 12 segments 4½″ wide

TRIPLE-STRIP SET 5 - - - - - - - - - - - - - - - - - - -

Make 2 strip sets for the square lap quilt or 3 for the square queen quilt. Subcut triplets 8, 10, and 13.

Note: If the usable width of fabric is only 40″, an additional strip set may be needed for the square queen quilt.

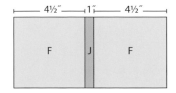

TRIPLE-STRIP SET 4 - - - - - - - -

Make 1 strip set for either quilt size. Subcut triplet 5.

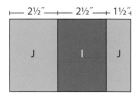

Square lap quilt

- Triplet 5: 4 segments 1″ wide

Square queen quilt

- Triplet 5: 6 segments 1″ wide

Square lap quilt

- Triplet 13: 4 segments 6½″ wide
- Triplet 8: 4 segments 2½″ wide
- Triplet 10: 8 segments 1½″ wide

Square queen quilt

- Triplet 13: 12 segments 6½″ wide
- Triplet 8: 6 segments 2½″ wide
- Triplet 10: 18 segments 1½″ wide

TRIPLE-STRIP SET 6

Make 1 strip set for the square lap quilt or 3 for the square queen quilt. Subcut triplets 9 and 14.

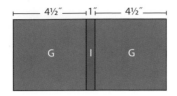

Square lap quilt

- Triplet 14: 2 segments 6½″ wide
- Triplet 9: 8 segments 2½″ wide

Square queen quilt

- Triplet 14: 6 segments 6½″ wide
- Triplet 9: 18 segments 2½″ wide

TRIPLE-STRIP SET 7

Make 1 strip set for the square lap quilt or 3 for the square queen quilt. Subcut triplet 11.

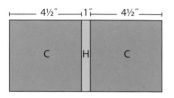

Square lap quilt

- Triplet 11: 8 segments 4½″ wide

Square queen quilt

- Triplet 11: 18 segments 4½″ wide

TRIPLE-STRIP SET 8

Make 1 strip set for either quilt size. Subcut triplet 12.

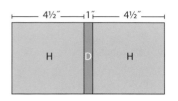

Square lap quilt

- Triplet 12: 4 segments 1″ wide

Square queen quilt

- Triplet 12: 9 segments 1″ wide

TRIPLE-STRIP SET 9

Make 2 strip sets for the square lap quilt or 5 for the square queen quilt. Subcut triplets 15, 17, and 20.

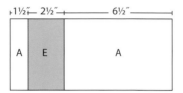

Square lap quilt

- Triplet 20: 4 segments 6½″ wide
- Triplet 15: 4 segments 2½″ wide
- Triplet 17: 8 segments 1½″ wide

Square queen quilt

- Triplet 20: 16 segments 6½″ wide
- Triplet 15: 8 segments 2½″ wide
- Triplet 17: 24 segments 1½″ wide

TRIPLE-STRIP SET 10

Make 1 strip set for the square lap quilt or 3 for the square queen quilt. Subcut triplets 16 and 21.

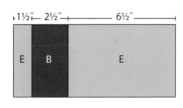

Square lap quilt

- Triplet 21: 2 segments 6½″ wide
- Triplet 16: 8 segments 2½″ wide

Square queen quilt

- Triplet 21: 8 segments 6½″ wide
- Triplet 16: 24 segments 2½″ wide

TRIPLE-STRIP SET 11

Make 1 strip set for the square lap quilt or 3 for the square queen quilt. Subcut triplet 18.

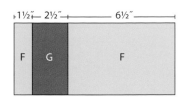

Square lap quilt

—Triplet 18: 8 segments 4½″ wide

Square queen quilt

—Triplet 18: 24 segments 4½″ wide

TRIPLE-STRIP SET 12

Make 1 strip set for either quilt size. Subcut triplet 19.

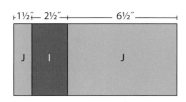

Square lap quilt

—Triplet 19: 4 segments 1″ wide

Square queen quilt

—Triplet 19: 12 segments 1″ wide

Quartets

QUADRUPLE-STRIP SET 1

Make 3 strip sets for the square lap quilt or 10 for the square queen quilt. Subcut quartets 1, 3, and 6.

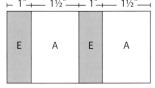

Square lap quilt

—Quartet 6: 8 segments 6½″ wide

—Quartet 1: 8 segments 2½″ wide

—Quartet 3: 24 segments 1½″ wide

Square queen quilt

—Quartet 6: 32 segments 6½″ wide

—Quartet 1: 16 segments 2½″ wide

—Quartet 3: 80 segments 1½″ wide

QUADRUPLE-STRIP SET 2

Make 2 strip sets for the square lap quilt or 6 for the square queen quilt. Subcut quartets 2, 7, and 8.

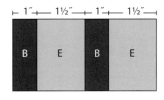

Square lap quilt

—Quartet 7: 4 segments 6½″ wide

—Quartet 2: 16 segments 2½″ wide

—Quartet 8 (for multi-rows): 8 segments 1″ wide

Square queen quilt

—Quartet 7: 8 segments 6½″ wide

—Quartet 2: 48 segments 2½″ wide

—Quartet 8 (for multi-rows): 32 segments 1″ wide

QUADRUPLE-STRIP SET 3

Make 2 strip sets for the square lap quilt or 6 for the square queen quilt. Subcut quartet 4.

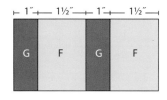

Square lap quilt

—Quartet 4: 16 segments 4½″ wide

Square queen quilt

—Quartet 4: 48 segments 4½″ wide

QUADRUPLE-STRIP SET 4

Make 1 strip set for either quilt size. Subcut quartet 5.

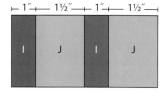

Square lap quilt

—Quartet 5: 8 segments 1″ wide

Square queen quilt

—Quartet 5: 24 segments 1″ wide

Connectors

Subcut connectors from the strips left over after you have made the strip sets.

FABRIC		CONNECTOR NUMBER	STRIP WIDTH	SUBCUT SEGMENTS THIS WIDE	QUANTITY	
					Square lap quilt	Square queen quilt
White/black merge (E)		3	6½"	6½"	2	8
		1	6½"	2½"	2	4
		2	6½"	1½"	4	12
Black (B)		5	6½"	6½"	1	4
		4	6½"	2½"	4	12
Black/orange merge (G)		6	4½"	6½"	4	12
Blue/black merge (I)		7	1"	6½"	2	6

Making the Multi-Rows

Being careful to pin at each seam junction, sew the designated quartets together *side to side* (not end to end) in the order indicated.

Make 2 multi-rows for the square lap quilt and 4 multi-rows for the square queen quilt. When you assemble the quilt, check twice to make sure you position the multi-rows correctly. The "inverted" multi-rows are exactly the same as the regular multi-rows; you just need to turn them upside down when you place them into the quilt.

To make the placement of the triplets and quartets easier to see, I grouped them in the following diagrams. Treat each finished multi-row as a single row.

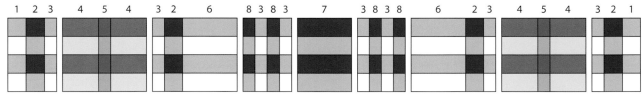

Square lap quilt multi-rows

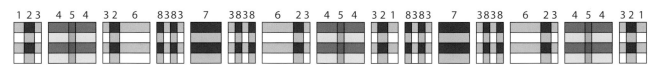

Square queen quilt multi-rows

Making the Rows

Referring to the Row Types table for your quilt size (below), sew the triplets, quartets, and connectors together to make each type of row. To sew each row together, start with the piece listed at the left and add each segment in order from left to right. The numbers in each column refer to the triplet, quartet, or connector number you made in Triplets, Quartets, and Connectors (page 65). Refer to How to Build a Tartan Design, Step 5 (page 20) for detailed instructions on how to assemble the rows. If the heading lists a segment as "inverse," be sure to sew it into the row in the opposite direction!

Row Types—Square Lap Quilt

ROW TYPE AND NUMBER TO MAKE	TRIPLET	TRIPLET	TRIPLET	QUARTET	CONNECTOR	INVERSE QUARTET	INVERSE TRIPLET	TRIPLET	INVERSE TRIPLET
A: Make 2.	1	8	15	1	1	1	15	8	1
B: Make 4.	2	9	16	2	4	2	16	9	2
C: Make 4.	3	10	17	3	2	3	17	10	3
D: Make 4.	4	11	18	4	6	4	18	11	4
E: Make 2.	5	12	19	5	7	5	19	12	5
F: Make 2.	6	13	20	6	3	6	20	13	6
G: Make 2.	Multi-row								
H: Make 1.	7	14	21	7	5	7	21	14	7

Row Types—Square Queen Quilt

ROW TYPE AND NUMBER TO MAKE	TRIPLET	TRIPLET	TRIPLET	QUARTET	CONNECTOR	INVERSE QUARTET	INVERSE TRIPLET	TRIPLET	TRIPLET	QUARTET	CONNECTOR	INVERSE QUARTET	INVERSE TRIPLET	TRIPLET	INVERSE TRIPLET
A: Make 2.	1	8	15	1	1	1	15	8	15	1	1	1	15	8	1
B: Make 6.	2	9	16	2	4	2	16	9	16	2	4	2	16	9	2
C: Make 6.	3	10	17	3	2	3	17	10	17	3	2	3	17	10	3
D: Make 6.	4	11	18	4	6	4	18	11	18	4	6	4	18	11	4
E: Make 2.	5	12	19	5	7	5	19	12	19	5	7	5	19	12	5
F: Make 4.	6	13	20	6	3	6	20	13	20	6	3	6	20	13	6
G: Make 4.	Multi-row														
H: Make 1.	7	14	21	7	5	7	21	14	21	7	5	7	21	14	7

Quilt Assembly

Referring to the quilt assembly diagrams (below and next page), sew the row types together in the indicated order to complete the quilt top. Press the seam allowances of each row in the opposite direction from adjacent rows. Pin at each and every seam intersection.

Row Number	Triplet	Triplet	Triplet	Quartet	*	Inverse Quartet	Inverse Triplet	Triplet	Inverse Triplet	Row Type
1	1	8	15	1	1	1	15	8	1	A
2	2	9	16	2	4	2	16	9	2	B
3	3	10	17	3	2	3	17	10	3	C
4	4	11	18	4	6	4	18	11	4	D
5	5	12	19	5	7	5	19	12	5	E
6	4	11	18	4	6	4	18	11	4	D
7	3	10	17	3	2	3	17	10	3	C
8	2	9	16	2	4	2	16	9	2	B
9	6	13	20	6	3	6	20	13	6	F
10										G
11	7	14	21	7	5	7	21	14	7	H
12										G
13	6	13	20	6	3	6	20	13	6	F
14	2	9	16	2	4	2	16	9	2	B
15	3	10	17	3	2	3	17	10	3	C
16	4	11	18	4	6	4	18	11	4	D
17	5	12	19	5	7	5	19	12	5	E
18	4	11	18	4	6	4	18	11	4	D
19	3	10	17	3	2	3	17	10	3	C
20	2	9	16	2	4	2	16	9	2	B
21	1	8	15	1	1	1	15	8	1	A

* Connector

Square lap quilt assembly

Row Number	Triplet	Triplet	Triplet	Quartet	*	Inverse Quartet	Inverse Triplet	Triplet	Triplet	Quartet	*	Inverse Quartet	Inverse Triplet	Triplet	Inverse Triplet	Row Type
1	1	8	15	1	1	1	15	8	15	1	1	1	15	8	1	A
2	2	9	16	2	4	2	16	9	16	2	4	2	16	9	2	B
3	3	10	17	3	2	3	17	10	17	3	2	3	17	10	3	C
4	4	11	18	4	6	4	18	11	18	4	6	4	18	11	4	D
5	5	12	19	5	7	5	19	12	19	5	7	5	19	12	5	E
6	4	11	18	4	6	4	18	11	18	4	6	4	18	11	4	D
7	3	10	17	3	2	3	17	10	17	3	2	3	17	10	3	C
8	2	9	16	2	4	2	16	9	16	2	4	2	16	9	2	B
9	6	13	20	6	3	6	20	13	20	6	3	6	20	13	6	F
10																G
11	7	14	21	7	5	7	21	14	21	7	5	7	21	14	7	H
12																G
13	6	13	20	6	3	6	20	13	20	6	3	6	20	13	6	F
14	2	9	16	2	4	2	16	9	16	2	4	2	16	9	2	B
15	3	10	17	3	2	3	17	10	17	3	2	3	17	10	3	C
16	4	11	18	4	6	4	18	11	18	4	6	4	18	11	4	D
17	5	12	19	5	7	5	19	12	19	5	7	5	19	12	5	E
18	4	11	18	4	6	4	18	11	18	4	6	4	18	11	4	D
19	3	10	17	3	2	3	17	10	17	3	2	3	17	10	3	C
20	2	9	16	2	4	2	16	9	16	2	4	2	16	9	2	B
21	6	13	20	6	3	6	20	13	20	6	3	6	20	13	6	F
22																G
23	7	14	21	7	5	7	21	14	21	7	5	7	21	14	7	H
24																G
25	6	13	20	6	3	6	20	13	20	6	3	6	20	13	6	F
26	2	9	16	2	4	2	16	9	16	2	4	2	16	9	2	B
27	3	10	17	3	2	3	17	10	17	3	2	3	17	10	3	C
28	4	11	18	4	6	4	18	11	18	4	6	4	18	11	4	D
29	5	12	19	5	7	5	19	12	19	5	7	5	19	12	5	E
30	4	11	18	4	6	4	18	11	18	4	6	4	18	11	4	D
31	1	8	15	1	1	1	15	8	15	1	1	1	15	8	1	C
32	2	9	16	2	4	2	16	9	16	2	4	2	16	9	2	B
33	3	10	17	3	2	3	17	10	17	3	2	3	17	10	3	A

* Connector

Square queen quilt assembly ---

Skill Level:
BEGINNER

MacRae of
Conchra

MacRae of Conchra square twin quilt, 78¼″ × 78¼″, made by Kathy Allen, quilted by Shannon Ryan-Freeman, 2016

The black/white merge in this traditionally colored quilt is a mint green that reads gray when combined with the other fabrics.

MacRae of Conchra table runner, 24¼″ × 51¼″, made by Kathy Allen, quilted by Shannon Ryan-Freeman, 2016

In this Christmas-themed table runner, the white base has been replaced with green, making thin stripes of red and green that intersect the main colors of white, gray, and black (all snowflake and star patterns).

MacRae of Conchra square lap quilt, 51¼″ × 51¼″, made by Kathy Allen, quilted by Shannon Ryan-Freeman, 2016

The neutral black, white, and gray are bisected by a thin red stripe. This quilt is true to the traditional colors of the MacRae of Conchra tartan. The use of Asian fabrics gives this quilt a subtle texture compared to those made with solid fabrics.

Eilean Donan Castle, located on an island in Loch Duich, was first built in the thirteenth century. It was the stronghold of the MacKenzies, and Clan MacRae served as constables. After the failed Jacobite uprising of 1719, the castle was held by the Spanish and was destroyed. By 1912, it was nothing but a pile of masonry. Then in 1911 John MacRae-Gilstrap purchased the castle, intending to preserve the ruins. Farquhar MacRae, a local stone mason, was hired to clear the site. When MacRae-Gilstrap returned from World War I, he found that Farquhar was in the process of restoring the castle, claiming he had seen what it originally looked like in a dream. John agreed to a full restoration of Eilean Donan Castle, and in 1932 it was complete. The castle opened to the public in 1955, thanks to the MacRaes of Conchra.

More than sixteen tartans are associated with Clan MacRae. My interpretation of the MacRae of Conchra tartan is a black-and-white pattern with thin stripes of red and yellow dissecting the larger squares. Although similar to the common tartan, the dissecting lines distinguish it. The more traditional MacRae of Conchra has dark blue instead of black.

	2"	3"	¾"	3"	3"	¾"	3"	3"	¾"	3"	2"	
	A	E	F	E	A	H	A	E	F	E	A	2"
	E	C	G	C	E	J	E	C	G	C	E	3"
	F	G	B	G	F	I	F	G	B	G	F	¾"
	E	C	G	C	E	J	E	C	G	C	E	3"
	A	E	F	E	A	H	A	E	F	E	A	3"
	H	J	I	J	H	D	H	J	I	J	H	¾"
	A	E	F	E	A	H	A	E	F	E	A	3"
	E	C	G	C	E	J	E	C	G	C	E	3"
	F	G	B	G	F	I	F	G	B	G	F	¾"
	E	C	G	C	E	J	E	C	G	C	E	3"
	A	E	F	E	A	H	A	E	F	E	A	2"

A single woven pattern in my interpretation of the MacRae of Conchra tartan. The *MacRae* quilts are created by repeating this pattern. The white (fabric A) is intersected by black (fabric C) to create the white/black merge (fabric E) in a checkered pattern. Thin stripes of red (fabrics D, H, and J) and yellow (fabrics B, F, and G) intersect through the black, white, and white/black merge blocks.

Materials

Yardages are listed for the table runner / square lap quilt / square twin quilt.

White (A): ½ yard / ¾ yard / 1⅝ yards

Yellow (B): ⅛ yard / ⅛ yard / ⅛ yard

Black (C): ½ yard / ¾ yard / 1½ yards

Red (D): ⅛ yard / ⅛ yard / ⅛ yard

White/black merge (E): ⅞ yard / 1⅜ yards / 3 yards

Yellow/white merge (F): ½ yard / ½ yard / ⅝ yard

Black/yellow merge (G): ⅜ yard / ½ yard / ¾ yard

White/red merge (H): ½ yard / ½ yard / ⅝ yard

Yellow/red merge (I): ⅛ yard / ⅛ yard / ⅛ yard

Black/red merge (J): ⅜ yard / ½ yard / ⅝ yard

Backing: 1¾ yards / 3½ yards / 7¼ yards (*Note:* If the usable fabric width is at least 44″, 5 yards will be enough for the square twin backing.)

Binding: ½ yard / ½ yard / ¾ yard (Black/red merge or white/red merge looks very good as the binding.)

TIP **Fabric Selection** The pattern of *MacRae* will show up better if fabric E, which will be the dominant fabric in this pattern, is a medium value that blends fabrics A and C. The fabrics that make up the thin stripe that intersects fabric A (fabrics D, H, I, and J), should be related to give a continuous color. In the sample, the fabrics are in the red family, which pops against the black and white fabrics. The fabrics that make up the thin stripe that intersects fabric C (fabrics B, F, and G) should also be related in color but more subtle. The differences in the two thin stripes will build the design.

Cutting

Cut all strips across the width of fabric. These strips will be used to create triple-strip sets and connectors. See How to Build a Tartan Design (page 16) for detailed instructions. Put a swatch of each fabric on the fabric organization worksheet (page 110) to help you keep your fabrics in order.

FABRIC		STRIP WIDTH	NUMBER OF STRIPS		
			Table runner	Square lap quilt	Square twin quilt
White (A)		3½″	3	5	12
		2½″	1	1	1
Yellow (B)		1¼″	1	1	2
Black (C)		3½″	4	6	14
Red (D)		1¼″	1	1	1
White/black merge (E)		3½″	7	13	26
Yellow/white merge (F)		3½″	2	2	2
		1¼″	3	4	7
Black/yellow merge (G)		3½″	2	2	4
		1¼″	2	3	7
White/red merge (H)		3½″	2	2	2
		2½″*	1	1	1
		1¼″	1	2	5
Yellow/red merge (I)		1¼″	2	2	2
Black/red merge (J)		3½″	2	2	2
		1¼″	1	3	6
Binding		2½″	5	6	9

For connectors only

Making the Quilt

Triplets and Connectors

Refer to the following lists to make strip sets from three fabrics for triple-strip sets. From the strip sets, subcut triplets.

Triplets

TRIPLE-STRIP SET 1 --

Make 2 strip sets for the table runner, 3 for the square lap quilt, or 6 for the square twin quilt. Subcut triplets 1 and 4.

Note: If the usable width of fabric is only 40″, an additional strip set may be needed for the square twin quilt.

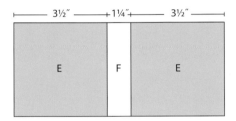

Table runner

⎡ Triplet 4: 12 segments 3½″ wide
⎣ Triplet 1: 4 segments 2½″ wide

Square lap quilt

⎡ Triplet 4: 24 segments 3½″ wide
⎣ Triplet 1: 8 segments 2½″ wide

Square twin quilt

⎡ Triplet 4: 60 segments 3½″ wide
⎣ Triplet 1: 12 segments 2½″ wide

TRIPLE-STRIP SET 2 --

Make 2 strip sets for the table runner, 3 for the square lap quilt, or 7 for the square twin quilt. Subcut triplet 2.

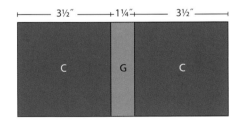

Table runner

— Triplet 2: 16 segments 3½″ wide

Square lap quilt

— Triplet 2: 32 segments 3½″ wide

Square twin quilt

— Triplet 2: 72 segments 3½″ wide

TRIPLE-STRIP SET 3 --

Make 1 strip set for the table runner or the square lap quilt or 2 for the square twin quilt. Subcut triplet 3.

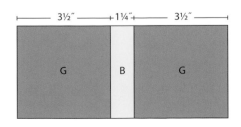

Table runner

— Triplet 3: 8 segments 1¼″ wide

Square lap quilt

— Triplet 3: 16 segments 1¼″ wide

Square twin quilt

— Triplet 3: 36 segments 1¼″ wide

TRIPLE-STRIP SET 4 -

Make 1 strip set for any project size.
Subcut triplet 5.

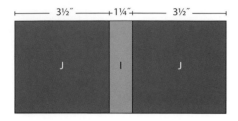

Table runner

—Triplet 5: 6 segments 1¼″ wide

Square lap quilt

—Triplet 5: 12 segments 1¼″ wide

Square twin quilt

—Triplet 5: 30 segments 1¼″ wide

TRIPLE-STRIP SET 5 -

Make 1 strip set for the table runner, 2 for the
square lap quilt, or 5 for the square twin quilt.
Subcut triplets 6 and 9.

Note: If the usable width of fabric is only 40″,
an additional strip set may be needed for the
square twin quilt.

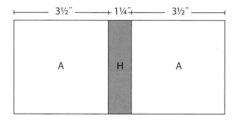

Table runner

┌ Triplet 9: 6 segments 3½″ wide

└ Triplet 6: 2 segments 2½″ wide

Square lap quilt

┌ Triplet 9: 18 segments 3½″ wide

└ Triplet 6: 6 segments 2½″ wide

Square twin quilt

┌ Triplet 9: 50 segments 3½″ wide

└ Triplet 6: 10 segments 2½″ wide

TRIPLE-STRIP SET 6 -

Make 1 strip set for the table runner, 3 for the
square lap quilt, or 6 for the square twin quilt.
Subcut triplet 7.

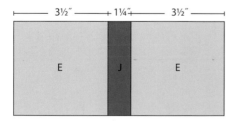

Table runner

—Triplet 7: 8 segments 3½″ wide

Square lap quilt

—Triplet 7: 24 segments 3½″ wide

Square twin quilt

—Triplet 7: 60 segments 3½″ wide

Make 1 strip set for any project size.

Subcut triplet 8.

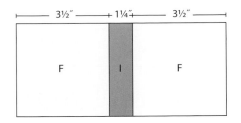

Table runner

—Triplet 8: 4 segments 1¼″ wide

Square lap quilt

—Triplet 8: 12 segments 1¼″ wide

Square twin quilt

—Triplet 8: 30 segments 1¼″ wide

TRIPLE-STRIP SET 8 -

Make 1 strip set for any project size.

Subcut triplet 10.

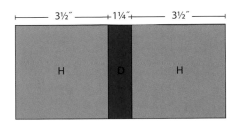

Table runner

—Triplet 10: 3 segments 1¼″ wide

Square lap quilt

—Triplet 10: 9 segments 1¼″ wide

Square twin quilt

—Triplet 10: 25 segments 1¼″ wide

Connectors

Subcut connectors from the strips left over after you have made the strip sets.

FABRIC		CONNECTOR NUMBER	STRIP WIDTH	SUBCUT SEGMENTS THIS WIDE	QUANTITY		
					Table runner	Square lap quilt	Square twin quilt
White (A)		4	3½″	2½″	12	12	20
		1	2½″	2½″	4	4	4
White/black merge (E)		2	3½″	2½″	16	16	24
Yellow/white merge (F)		3	1¼″	2½″	8	8	12
White/red merge (H)		5	2½″	1¼″	6	6	10

TIP ▸ **Palindromes** The triplets and rows of *MacRae* are all palindromes (reading the same forward and backward), so you don't have to be careful about how you sew them into the rows. But recheck the seam allowances in each row to be sure they are all pointed the same way, in alternating directions from row to row.

Making the Rows

Referring to the Row Types table for your quilt size (below), sew the triplets and connectors together to make each type of row. To sew each row together, start with the piece listed at the left and add each segment in order from left to right. The numbers in each column refer to the triplet or connector number you made in Triplets and Connectors (page 77). Refer to How to Build a Tartan Design, Step 5 (page 20) for detailed instructions on how to assemble the rows.

TIP **Triplet 4 and Triplet 7** These triplets are very close in appearance. Be careful not to mix them up!

Row Types—Table Runner

ROW TYPE AND NUMBER TO MAKE	CONNECTOR	TRIPLET	TRIPLET	TRIPLET	CONNECTOR
A: Make 2.	1	1	6	1	1
B: Make 8.	2	2	7	2	2
C: Make 4.	3	3	8	3	3
D: Make 6.	4	4	9	4	4
E: Make 3.	5	5	10	5	5

Row Types—Square Lap Quilt

ROW TYPE AND NUMBER TO MAKE	CONNECTOR	TRIPLET	TRIPLET	TRIPLET	TRIPLET	TRIPLET	TRIPLET	TRIPLET	CONNECTOR
A: Make 2.	1	1	6	1	6	1	6	1	1
B: Make 8.	2	2	7	2	7	2	7	2	2
C: Make 4.	3	3	8	3	8	3	8	3	3
D: Make 6.	4	4	9	4	9	4	9	4	4
E: Make 3.	5	5	10	5	10	5	10	5	5

Row Types—Square Twin Quilt

ROW TYPE AND NUMBER TO MAKE	CONNECTOR	TRIPLET	TRIPLET	TRIPLET	TRIPLET	TRIPLET	TRIPLET	TRIPLET	TRIPLET	TRIPLET	TRIPLET	CONNECTOR
A: Make 2.	1	1	6	1	6	1	6	1	6	1	6	1	1
B: Make 12.	2	2	7	2	7	2	7	2	7	2	7	2	2
C: Make 6.	3	3	8	3	8	3	8	3	8	3	8	3	3
D: Make 10.	4	4	9	4	9	4	9	4	9	4	9	4	4
E: Make 5.	5	5	10	5	10	5	10	5	10	5	10	5	5

Table runner assembly

Row Number	*	Triplet	Triplet	Triplet	*	Row Type
1	1	1	6	1	1	A
2	2	2	7	2	2	B
3	3	3	8	3	3	C
4	2	2	7	2	2	B
5	4	4	9	4	4	D
6	5	5	10	5	5	E
7	4	4	9	4	4	D
8	2	2	7	2	2	B
9	3	3	8	3	3	C
10	2	2	7	2	2	B
11	4	4	9	4	4	D
12	5	5	10	5	5	E
13	4	4	9	4	4	D
14	2	2	7	2	2	B
15	3	3	8	3	3	C
16	2	2	7	2	2	B
17	4	4	9	4	4	D
18	5	5	10	5	5	E
19	4	4	9	4	4	D
20	2	2	7	2	2	B
21	3	3	8	3	3	C
22	2	2	7	2	2	B
23	1	1	6	1	1	A

* Connector

Quilt Assembly

Referring to the quilt assembly diagrams (at left, below, and page 82), sew the row types together in the indicated order to complete the quilt top. Press the seam allowances of each row in the opposite direction from adjacent rows. Pin at each and every seam intersection.

Square lap quilt assembly

Row Number	*	Triplet	Triplet	Triplet	Triplet	Triplet	Triplet	Triplet	*	Row Type
1	1	1	6	1	6	1	6	1	1	A
2	2	2	7	2	7	2	7	2	2	B
3	3	3	8	3	8	3	8	3	3	C
4	2	2	7	2	7	2	7	2	2	B
5	4	4	9	4	9	4	9	4	4	D
6	5	5	10	5	10	5	10	5	5	E
7	4	4	9	4	9	4	9	4	4	D
8	2	2	7	2	7	2	7	2	2	B
9	3	3	8	3	8	3	8	3	3	C
10	2	2	7	2	7	2	7	2	2	B
11	4	4	9	4	9	4	9	4	4	D
12	5	5	10	5	10	5	10	5	5	E
13	4	4	9	4	9	4	9	4	4	D
14	2	2	7	2	7	2	7	2	2	B
15	3	3	8	3	8	3	8	3	3	C
16	2	2	7	2	7	2	7	2	2	B
17	4	4	9	4	9	4	9	4	4	D
18	5	5	10	5	10	5	10	5	5	E
19	4	4	9	4	9	4	9	4	4	D
20	2	2	7	2	7	2	7	2	2	B
21	3	3	8	3	8	3	8	3	3	C
22	2	2	7	2	7	2	7	2	2	B
23	1	1	6	1	6	1	6	1	1	A

* Connector

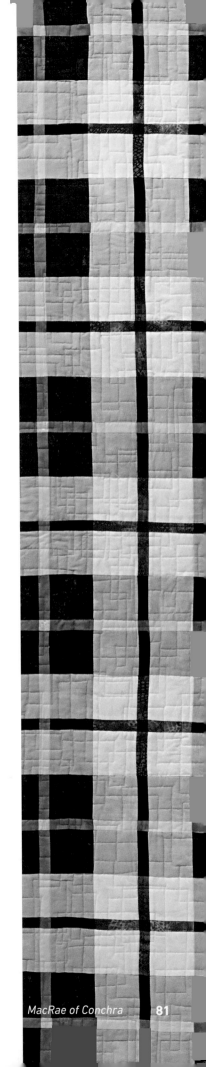

Square twin quilt assembly chart — Row assembly with 10 Triplet columns.

Row Number	*	Triplet	Triplet	Triplet	Triplet	Triplet	Triplet	Triplet	Triplet	Triplet	Triplet	*	Row Type
1	1	1	6	1	6	1	6	1	6	1	6	1	A
2	2	2	7	2	7	2	7	2	7	2	7	2	B
3	3	3	8	3	8	3	8	3	8	3	8	3	C
4	2	2	7	2	7	2	7	2	7	2	7	2	B
5	4	4	9	4	9	4	9	4	9	4	9	4	D
6	5	5	10	5	10	5	10	5	10	5	10	5	E
7	4	4	9	4	9	4	9	4	9	4	9	4	D
8	2	2	7	2	7	2	7	2	7	2	7	2	B
9	3	3	8	3	8	3	8	3	8	3	8	3	C
10	2	2	7	2	7	2	7	2	7	2	7	2	B
11	4	4	9	4	9	4	9	4	9	4	9	4	D
12	5	5	10	5	10	5	10	5	10	5	10	5	E
13	4	4	9	4	9	4	9	4	9	4	9	4	D
14	2	2	7	2	7	2	7	2	7	2	7	2	B
15	3	3	8	3	8	3	8	3	8	3	8	3	C
16	2	2	7	2	7	2	7	2	7	2	7	2	B
17	4	4	9	4	9	4	9	4	9	4	9	4	D
18	5	5	10	5	10	5	10	5	10	5	10	5	E
19	4	4	9	4	9	4	9	4	9	4	9	4	D
20	2	2	7	2	7	2	7	2	7	2	7	2	B
21	3	3	8	3	8	3	8	3	8	3	8	3	C
22	2	2	7	2	7	2	7	2	7	2	7	2	B
23	4	4	9	4	9	4	9	4	9	4	9	4	D
24	5	5	10	5	10	5	10	5	10	5	10	5	E
25	4	4	9	4	9	4	9	4	9	4	9	4	D
26	2	2	7	2	7	2	7	2	7	2	7	2	B
27	3	3	8	3	8	3	8	3	8	3	8	3	C
28	2	2	7	2	7	2	7	2	7	2	7	2	B
29	4	4	9	4	9	4	9	4	9	4	9	4	D
30	5	5	10	5	10	5	10	5	10	5	10	5	E
31	4	4	9	4	9	4	9	4	9	4	9	4	D
32	2	2	7	2	7	2	7	2	7	2	7	2	B
33	3	3	8	3	8	3	8	3	8	3	8	3	C
34	2	2	7	2	7	2	7	2	7	2	7	2	B
35	1	1	6	1	6	1	6	1	6	1	6	1	A

Square twin quilt assembly

* Connector

Skill Level:
EXPERIENCED

Fraser

Fraser square lap quilt, 65½″ × 65½″, made by Kathy Allen, quilted by Shannon Ryan-Freeman, 2017

The green and blue patterns on the gray background are bisected by alternating thin red and white stripes. The traditional colors of the Fraser hunting tartan are blues and greens of similar value against a dark gray background.

The Frasers have a long and heroic family history in their battles against the English. They participated in every major military conflict, and their loyalty and relation to Robert the Bruce brought both fame and martyrdom to the chiefs of this clan. (Sir Simon Fraser was executed in 1306 in the same horrible manner as his friend, William Wallace.) Their alliance with Charles Edward Stuart (Bonnie Prince Charlie) during the Jacobite war of 1746 has been documented (and romanticized) in the book series Outlander by Diana Gabaldon.

The Frasers (particularly the Frasers of Lovat) have also been known to take power struggles to a new level. When the ninth Lord Lovat died unexpectedly in 1696, his eldest daughter, Amelia, was offered to Thomas of Beaufort, who took on the name tenth Lord Lovat. While all these formalities were taking place, Beaufort's son, Simon, kidnapped the young widow of the ninth Lord Lovat, dragging her to a drunken priest who married them. The marriage was then consummated in the presence of the priest, to make sure it was a legal and binding marriage. The Privy Council, comprised of family members of the young widow who was now married to Simon, were outraged by this and convicted him of treason. Thomas Beaufort was horrified by the treatment of his son and fled to Skye, where he died a year later. Simon Beaufort then became the eleventh Lord Lovat in 1698, proving that devious force can sometimes work. 50 years later, the eleventh Lord Lovat was beheaded in London, after the disastrous Jacobite War of 1746.

The stunning Fraser tartan has a background of dark gray with large strips of blue and green. The tiny strips of white and red that run on the outside of the blue and green strips set this tartan off. To make the strips stand out, fabrics B, F, J, M, and O should all be very light values and fabrics E, I, J, K, and L should all be in the red family.

3"	1"	3"	2½"	½"	3"	½"	3"	½"	2½"	3"	½"	3"	
A	F	A	G	A	H	A	H	A	G	A	I	A	3"
I	J	I	K	I	L	I	L	I	K	I	E	I	1"
A	F	A	G	A	H	A	H	A	G	A	I	A	3"
G	M	G	C	G	N	G	N	G	C	G	K	G	2½"
A	F	A	G	A	H	A	H	A	G	A	I	A	½"
H	O	H	N	H	D	H	D	H	N	H	L	H	3"
A	F	A	G	A	H	A	H	A	G	A	I	A	½"
H	O	H	N	H	D	H	D	H	N	H	L	H	3"
A	F	A	G	A	H	A	H	A	G	A	I	A	½"
G	M	G	C	G	N	G	N	G	C	G	K	G	2½"
A	F	A	G	A	H	A	H	A	G	A	I	A	3"
F	B	F	M	F	O	F	O	F	M	F	J	F	½"
A	F	A	G	A	H	A	H	A	G	A	I	A	3"

A single woven pattern in my interpretation of the Fraser hunting tartan. The Fraser tartan is created by repeating this pattern. The background (fabric A) is of the same value as the bisected sixteen-patch made of blues and greens. What makes this pattern stand out are the thin alternating red (fabrics E, I, J, K, and L) and white (fabrics B, F, J, M, and O) stripes.

Materials

Yardages are listed for the square lap quilt.

Dark gray (A): 1¼ yards

White (B): ⅛ yard

Green (C): ⅜ yard

Blue (D): ½ yard

Red (E): ⅛ yard

White/gray merge (F): ¾ yard

Gray/green merge (G): 1¼ yards

Blue/gray merge (H): 1¾ yards

Gray/red merge (I): ¾ yard

Red/white merge (J): ⅛ yard

Green/red merge (K): ¼ yard

Red/blue merge (L): ½ yard

White/green merge (M): ¼ yard

Blue/green merge (N): 1 yard

White/blue merge (O): ½ yard

Backing: 4¼ yards

Binding: ¾ yards

Fraser hunting tartan
in modern colors

Cutting

Cut all strips across the width of fabric. These strips will be used to create quadruple-strip sets, triple-strip sets, and connectors. See How to Build a Tartan Design (page 16) for detailed instructions. Put a swatch of each fabric on the fabric organization worksheet (page 110) to help you keep your fabrics in order.

FABRIC		STRIP WIDTH	NUMBER OF STRIPS
			Square lap quilt
Dark gray (A)		3½"	8
		1"	9
White (B)		1½"	1
Green (C)		3"	3
Blue (D)		3½"	4
Red (E)		1½"	1
White/gray merge (F)		3½"	4
		1½"	2
		1"	2
Gray/green merge (G)		3½"	4
		3"	6
		1"	5
Blue/gray merge (H)		3½"	14
		1"	6
Gray/red merge (I)		3½"	4
		1½"	2
		1"	2
Red/white merge (J)		1½"	2
Green/red merge (K)		3"	1
		1½"	1
Red/blue merge (L)		3½"	2
		1½"	2
White/green merge (M)		3"	1
		1½"	1
Blue/green merge (N)		3½"	4
		3"	4
White/blue merge (O)		3½"	2
		1½"	2
Binding		2½"	8

TIPS ◆ Organizing Your Fabrics

• *Fraser* has fifteen fabrics used to create eighteen different triplets (from fifteen different triple-strip sets) and six doublets (from five different double-strip sets). Use the fabric organization worksheet (page 110) to help keep the fabrics organized. And use your favorite method to label all the triplets!

• The gray/green merge (fabric G) has strips cut into 3″ and 3½″ widths. Be sure to select the right strip size when constructing triple-strip sets 3 and 13 and double-strip set 1.

Making the Quilt

Triplets and Doublets

Refer to the following lists to make strip sets from three fabrics for triple-strip sets or two fabrics for double-strip sets. From the strip sets, subcut triplets and doublets.

Triplets

TRIPLE-STRIP SET 1

Make 2 strip sets. Subcut triplets 1 and 4.

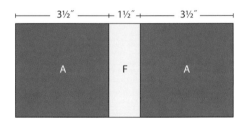

— **Triplet 1:** 16 segments 3½″ wide

— **Triplet 4:** 18 segments 1″ wide

TRIPLE-STRIP SET 2

Make 1 strip set. Subcut triplet 2.

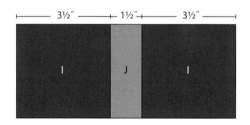

— **Triplet 2:** 4 segments 1½″ wide

TRIPLE-STRIP SET 3

Make 1 strip set. Subcut triplet 3.

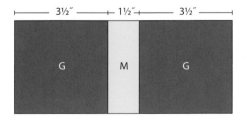

— **Triplet 3:** 12 segments 3″ wide

TRIPLE-STRIP SET 4

Make 2 strip sets. Subcut triplet 5.

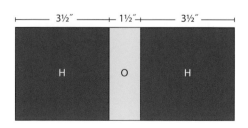

— **Triplet 5:** 12 segments 3½″ wide

TRIPLE-STRIP SET 5
Make 1 strip set. Subcut triplet 6.

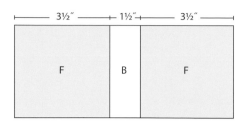

—**Triplet 6:** 4 segments 1½″ wide

TRIPLE-STRIP SET 6
Make 3 strip sets.
Subcut triplets 7 and 10.

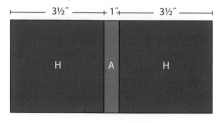

┌ **Triplet 7:** 24 segments 3½″ wide
└ **Triplet 10:** 27 segments 1″ wide

TRIPLE-STRIP SET 7
Make 1 strip set. Subcut triplet 8.

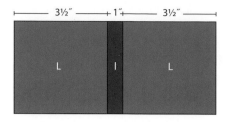

—**Triplet 8:** 6 segments 1½″ wide

TRIPLE-STRIP SET 8
Make 2 strip sets. Subcut triplet 9.

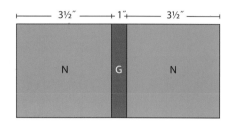

—**Triplet 9:** 18 segments 3″ wide

TRIPLE-STRIP SET 9
Make 2 strip sets. Subcut triplet 11.

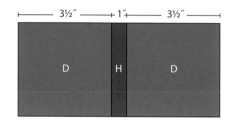

—**Triplet 11:** 18 segments 3½″ wide

TRIPLE-STRIP SET 10
Make 1 strip set. Subcut triplet 12.

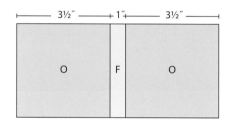

—**Triplet 12:** 6 segments 1½″ wide

TRIPLE-STRIP SET 11
Make 2 strip sets. Subcut triplets 13 and 16.

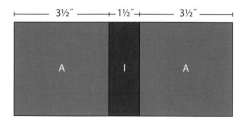

┌ **Triplet 13:** 16 segments 3½″ wide
└ **Triplet 16:** 18 segments 1″ wide

TRIPLE-STRIP SET 12
Make 1 strip set. Subcut triplet 14.

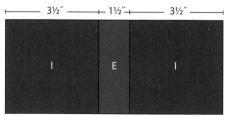

—**Triplet 14:** 4 segments 1½″ wide

TRIPLE-STRIP SET 13
Make 1 strip set. Subcut triplet 15.

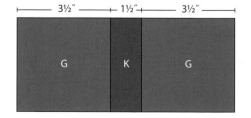

—**Triplet 15:** 12 segments 3″ wide

TRIPLE-STRIP SET 14

Make 2 strip sets. Subcut triplet 17.

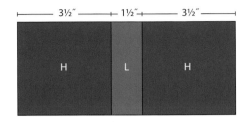

├─ 3½″ ─┤├ 1½″ ┤├─ 3½″ ─┤

—**Triplet 17:** 12 segments 3½″ wide

TRIPLE-STRIP SET 15

Make 1 strip set. Subcut triplet 18.

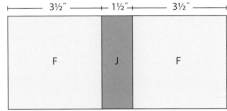

├─ 3½″ ─┤├ 1½″ ┤├─ 3½″ ─┤

—**Triplet 18:** 4 segments 1½″ wide

Doublets

DOUBLE-STRIP SET 1

Make 6 strip sets. Subcut doublets 1 and 4.

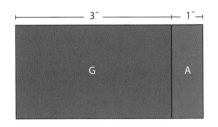

├─── 3″ ───┤├ 1″ ┤

┌ **Doublet 1:** 48 segments 3½″ wide

└ **Doublet 4:** 54 segments 1″ wide

DOUBLE-STRIP SET 2

Make 1 strip set. Subcut doublet 2.

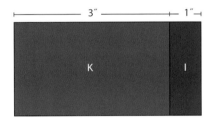

├─── 3″ ───┤├ 1″ ┤

—**Doublet 2:** 12 segments 1½″ wide

DOUBLE-STRIP SET 3

Make 3 strip sets. Subcut doublet 3.

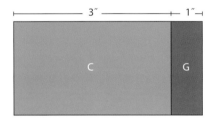

├─── 3″ ───┤├ 1″ ┤

—**Doublet 3:** 36 segments 3″ wide

DOUBLE-STRIP SET 4

Make 4 strip sets. Subcut doublet 5.

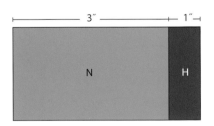

├─── 3″ ───┤├ 1″ ┤

—**Doublet 5:** 36 segments 3½″ wide

DOUBLE-STRIP SET 5

Make 1 strip set. Subcut doublet 6.

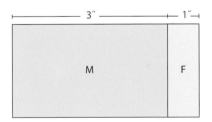

├─── 3″ ───┤├ 1″ ┤

—**Doublet 6:** 12 segments 1½″ wide

Making the Rows

Referring to the Row Types table (below), sew the triplets and doublets together to make each type of row. To sew each row together, start with the piece listed at the left and add each segment in order from left to right. The numbers in each column refer to the triplet or doublet number you made in Triplets and Doublets (page 87). Refer to How to Build a Tartan Design, Step 5 (page 20) for detailed instructions on how to assemble the rows. If the heading lists a segment as "inverse," be sure to sew it into the row in the opposite direction!

NOTE

Caution! *Unlike most of the other tartans in this book, the rows in this pattern are not palindromes (reading the same forward and backward). Be sure to pay attention to which direction they should be sewn into the quilt.*

Row Types—Square Lap Quilt

ROW TYPE AND NUMBER TO MAKE	TRIPLET	DOUBLET	TRIPLET	INVERSE DOUBLET	TRIPLET	DOUBLET	TRIPLET	INVERSE DOUBLET	TRIPLET	DOUBLET	TRIPLET	INVERSE DOUBLET	TRIPLET
A: Make 8.	1	1	7	1	13	1	7	1	1	1	7	1	13
B: Make 2.	2	2	8	2	14	2	8	2	2	2	8	2	14
C: Make 6.	3	3	9	3	15	3	9	3	3	3	9	3	15
D: Make 9.	4	4	10	4	16	4	10	4	4	4	10	4	16
E: Make 6.	5	5	11	5	17	5	11	5	5	5	11	5	17
F: Make 2.	6	6	12	6	18	6	12	6	6	6	12	6	18

Quilt Assembly

Referring to the quilt assembly diagram, sew the row types together in the indicated order to complete the quilt top. Press the seam allowances of each row in the opposite direction from adjacent rows. Pin at each and every seam intersection.

Row Number	Triplet	Doublet	Triplet	Inverse Doublet	Triplet	Doublet	Triplet	Inverse Doublet	Triplet	Doublet	Triplet	Inverse Doublet	Triplet	Row Type
1	1	1	7	1	13	1	7	1	1	1	7	1	13	A
2	2	2	8	2	14	2	8	2	2	2	8	2	14	B
3	1	1	7	1	13	1	7	1	1	1	7	1	13	A
4	3	3	9	3	15	3	9	3	3	3	9	3	15	C
5	4	4	10	4	16	4	10	4	4	4	10	4	16	D
6	5	5	11	5	17	5	11	5	5	5	11	5	17	E
7	4	4	10	4	16	4	10	4	4	4	10	4	16	D
8	5	5	11	5	17	5	11	5	5	5	11	5	17	E
9	4	4	10	4	16	4	10	4	4	4	10	4	16	D
10	3	3	9	3	15	3	9	3	3	3	9	3	15	C
11	1	1	7	1	13	1	7	1	1	1	7	1	13	A
12	6	6	12	6	18	6	12	6	6	6	12	6	18	F
13	1	1	7	1	13	1	7	1	1	1	7	1	13	A
14	3	3	9	3	15	3	9	3	3	3	9	3	15	C
15	4	4	10	4	16	4	10	4	4	4	10	4	16	D
16	5	5	11	5	17	5	11	5	5	5	11	5	17	E
17	4	4	10	4	16	4	10	4	4	4	10	4	16	D
18	5	5	11	5	17	5	11	5	5	5	11	5	17	E
19	4	4	10	4	16	4	10	4	4	4	10	4	16	D
20	3	3	9	3	15	3	9	3	3	3	9	3	15	C
21	1	1	7	1	13	1	7	1	1	1	7	1	13	A
22	2	2	8	2	14	2	8	2	2	2	8	2	14	B
23	1	1	7	1	13	1	7	1	1	1	7	1	13	A
24	3	3	9	3	15	3	9	3	3	3	9	3	15	C
25	4	4	10	4	16	4	10	4	4	4	10	4	16	D
26	5	5	11	5	17	5	11	5	5	5	11	5	17	E
27	4	4	10	4	16	4	10	4	4	4	10	4	16	D
28	5	5	11	5	17	5	11	5	5	5	11	5	17	E
29	4	4	10	4	16	4	10	4	4	4	10	4	16	D
30	3	3	9	3	15	3	9	3	3	3	9	3	15	C
31	1	1	7	1	13	1	7	1	1	1	7	1	13	A
32	6	6	12	6	18	6	12	6	6	6	12	6	18	F
33	1	1	7	1	13	1	7	1	1	1	7	1	13	A

Quilt assembly

Skill Level: **INTERMEDIATE**

Amador

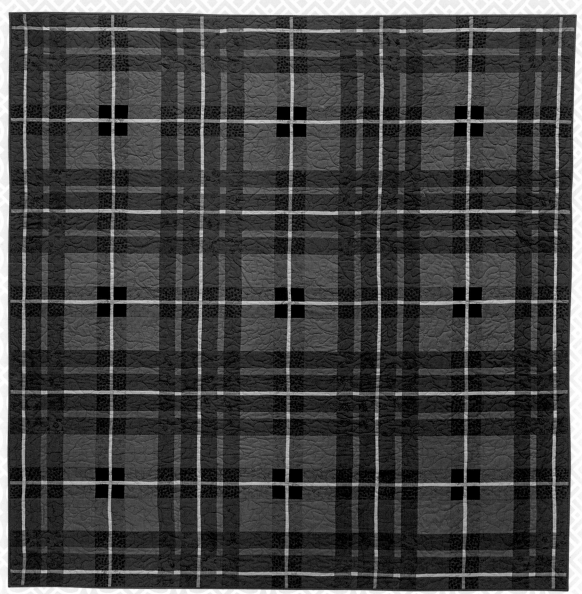

Amador square full quilt, 85½″ × 85½″, made by Kathy Allen, quilted by Shannon Ryan-Freeman, 2017

Made completely with Simply Primitive, a new collection by Batik Textiles, the dominant colors of army green and tan show the latticed pattern, which is then dissected by the thin light-value stripes that make this version of the Amador pattern distinctive.

Amador table runner, 31½″ × 58½″, made by Kathy Allen, quilted by Shannon Ryan-Freeman, 2017

By replacing black with purple and selecting a tan/green merge fabric that included purple in its design, this table runner conveys the spring season.

Amador square lap quilt, 58½″ × 58½″, made by Kathy Allen, quilted by Shannon Ryan-Freeman, 2016

Polka-dotted greens crisscross against a tan background. The greens, despite their lack of traditionally complementary hues, work together.

Amador County, for which this pattern is named, is located in the Sierra Nevada foothills of California. This region has a rich history associated with California's gold rush and the Kennedy, Eureka, and Argonaut mines. From all around the world, hopeful miners flocked to the hills at the base of the majestic Sierras. It is from the wealth mined in Amador that San Francisco was built. California may have been conceived in Coloma, where gold was first discovered, but California was born in Amador, where millions of dollars in gold were mined.

The Amador tartan, one of my own design, is a mix of the four basic colors: yellow, green, black, and tan. It is unusual in that the outer lines of the single pattern are separated by a very thin stripe of yellow, so that multi-pattern projects will create a dominant green at the corners and borders.

TIP Fabric Selection

To make the multi-strip pattern show, fabrics C, G, and J should be the lowest-value fabrics, with fabric C being the darkest. The green fabrics, which will give the quilt its definition, are fabrics B, G, and I. The background is fabric D, and its value should be light enough to not interfere with the fabrics that make up the pattern.

A single woven pattern in my Amador tartan design. The *Amador* quilts are created by repeating this pattern. There are two distinct patterns over a background of tan: The dark brown crisscross creates a double tic-tac-toe when the four patterns are put together, and the green corners come together with neighboring green corners to give this tartan its primary color.

2″	½″	2½″	1″	2½″	5″	2″	½″	2″	5″	2½″	1″	2½″	½″	2″	
B	E	B	I	B	I	G	E	G	I	B	I	B	E	B	2″
E	A	E	H	E	H	F	A	F	H	E	H	E	A	E	½″
B	E	B	I	B	I	G	E	G	I	B	I	B	E	B	2½″
I	H	I	D	I	D	J	H	J	D	I	D	I	H	I	1″
B	E	B	I	B	I	G	E	G	I	B	I	B	E	B	2½″
I	H	I	D	I	D	J	H	J	D	I	D	I	H	I	5″
G	F	G	J	G	J	C	F	C	J	G	J	G	F	G	2″
E	A	E	H	E	H	F	A	F	H	E	H	E	A	E	½″
G	F	G	J	G	J	C	F	C	J	G	J	G	F	G	2″
I	H	I	D	I	D	J	H	J	D	I	D	I	H	I	5″
B	E	B	I	B	I	G	E	G	I	B	I	B	E	B	2½″
I	H	I	D	I	D	J	H	J	D	I	D	I	H	I	1″
B	E	B	I	B	I	G	E	G	I	B	I	B	E	B	2½″
E	A	E	H	E	H	F	A	F	H	E	H	E	A	E	½″
B	E	B	I	B	I	G	E	G	I	B	I	B	E	B	2″

Materials

Yardages are listed for the table runner / square lap quilt / square full quilt.

Yellow (A): ⅛ yard / ⅛ yard / ⅛ yard

Green (B): ⅝ yard / 1 yard / 1⅝ yards

Black (C): ¼ yard / ¼ yard / ⅜ yard

Tan (D): ⅝ yard / 1 yard / 1⅞ yards

Yellow/green merge (E): ⅜ yard / ⅝ yard / ⅞ yard

Yellow/black merge (F): ⅜ yard / ⅜ yard / ½ yard

Green/black merge (G): ½ yard / ⅞ yard / 1¼ yards

Yellow/tan merge (H): ¼ yard / ⅜ yard / ⅞ yard

Green/tan merge (I): 1 yard / 1¾ yards / 3½ yards

Black/tan merge (J): ½ yard / ¾ yard / 1¼ yards

Backing: 2 yards / 3¾ yards / 8 yards

Binding: ½ yard / ¾ yard / 1 yard (Black/tan merge looks good as a binding.)

Cutting

Cut all strips across the width of fabric. These strips will be used to create quadruple-strip sets, triple-strip sets, and connectors. See How to Build a Tartan Design (page 16) for detailed instructions. Put a swatch of each fabric on the fabric organization worksheet (page 110) to help you keep your fabrics in order.

FABRIC		STRIP WIDTH	NUMBER OF STRIPS		
			Table runner	Square lap quilt	Square full quilt
Yellow (A)		1″	2	2	2
Green (B)		3″	4	8	16
		2½″*	2	2	3
Black (C)		2½″	2	2	4
Tan (D)		5½″	2	3	8
		1½″	2	4	8
Yellow/green merge (E)		3″	2	4	4
		1″	4	6	10
Yellow/black merge (F)		2½″	2	2	2
		1″	2	2	4
Green/black merge (G)		3″	2	4	6
		2½″	3	5	9
Yellow/tan merge (H)		5½″	0	0	1
		1½″	1	2	2
		1″	5	8	13
Green/tan merge (I)		5½″	0	0	3
		3″	7	13	23
		2½″*	2	3	4
		1½″	2	4	8
Black/tan merge (J)		5½″	0	0	1
		2½″	4	7	12
		1½″	1	2	3
Binding		2½″	5	7	10

* For connectors only

Making the Quilt

Triplets, Quartets, and Connectors

Refer to the following lists to make strip sets from three fabrics for triple-strip sets or four fabrics for quadruple-strip sets. From the strip sets, subcut triplets and quartets.

Quartets

QUADRUPLE-STRIP SET 1

Make 2 strip sets for the table runner, 3 for the square lap quilt, or 5 for the square full quilt. Subcut quartets 1 and 3.

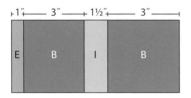

Table runner

- Quartet 3: 16 segments 3″ wide
- Quartet 1: 4 segments 2½″ wide

Square lap quilt

- Quartet 3: 24 segments 3″ wide
- Quartet 1: 6 segments 2½″ wide

Square full quilt

- Quartet 3: 48 segments 3″ wide
- Quartet 1: 8 segments 2½″ wide

QUADRUPLE-STRIP SET 2

Make 1 strip set for any project size. Subcut quartet 2.

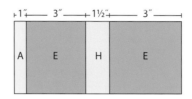

Table runner

- Quartet 2: 10 segments 1″ wide

Square lap quilt

- Quartet 2: 15 segments 1″ wide

Square full quilt

- Quartet 2: 28 segments 1″ wide

QUADRUPLE-STRIP SET 3

Make 2 strip sets for the table runner, 3 for the square lap quilt, or 5 for the square full quilt. Subcut quartets 4 and 5.

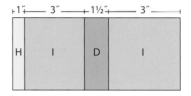

Table runner

- Quartet 5: 8 segments 5½″ wide
- Quartet 4: 8 segments 1½″ wide

Square lap quilt

- Quartet 5: 12 segments 5½″ wide
- Quartet 4: 12 segments 1½″ wide

Square full quilt

- Quartet 5: 24 segments 5½″ wide
- Quartet 4: 24 segments 1½″ wide

QUADRUPLE-STRIP SET 4

Make 1 strip set for the table runner or the square lap quilt or 2 for the square full quilt. Subcut quartet 6.

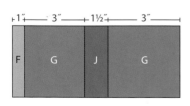

Table runner

- Quartet 6: 8 segments 2½″ wide

Square lap quilt

- Quartet 6: 12 segments 2½″ wide

Square full quilt

- Quartet 6: 24 segments 2½″ wide

QUADRUPLE-STRIP SET 5

Make 3 strip sets for the square full quilt only. Subcut quartets 7 and 9.

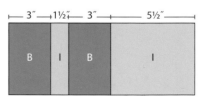

Square full quilt

- Quartet 9: 24 segments 3″ wide
- Quartet 7: 4 segments 2½″ wide

QUADRUPLE-STRIP SET 6

Make 1 strip set for the square full quilt only. Subcut quartet 8.

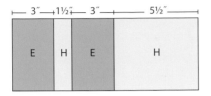

Square full quilt

—Quartet 8: 14 segments 1″ wide

QUADRUPLE-STRIP SET 7

Make 3 strip sets for the square full quilt only. Subcut quartets 10 and 11.

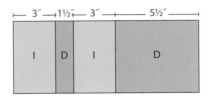

Square full quilt

┌Quartet 11: 12 segments 5½″ wide

└Quartet 10: 12 segments 1½″ wide

QUADRUPLE-STRIP SET 8

Make 1 strip set for the square full quilt only. Subcut quartet 12.

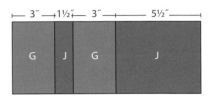

Square full quilt

—Quartet 12: 12 segments 2½″ wide

Triplets

TRIPLE-STRIP SET 1

Make 1 strip set for the table runner, 2 for the square lap quilt, or 4 for the square full quilt. Subcut triplets 1 and 3.

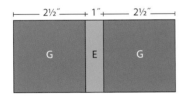

Table runner

┌Triplet 3: 8 segments 3″ wide

└Triplet 1: 2 segments 2½″ wide

Square lap quilt

┌Triplet 3: 16 segments 3″ wide

└Triplet 1: 4 segments 2½″ wide

Square full quilt

┌Triplet 3: 36 segments 3″ wide

└Triplet 1: 6 segments 2½″ wide

TRIPLE-STRIP SET 2

Make 1 strip set for any project size. Subcut triplet 2.

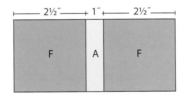

Table runner

—Triplet 2: 5 segments 1″ wide

Square lap quilt

—Triplet 2: 10 segments 1″ wide

Square full quilt

—Triplet 2: 21 segments 1″ wide

TRIPLE-STRIP SET 3

Make 1 strip set for the table runner, 2 for the square lap quilt, or 4 for the square full quilt. Subcut triplets 4 and 5.

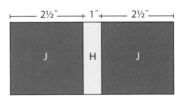

Table runner

┌Triplet 5: 4 segments 5½″ wide

└Triplet 4: 4 segments 1½″ wide

Square lap quilt

┌Triplet 5: 8 segments 5½″ wide

└Triplet 4: 8 segments 1½″ wide

Square full quilt

┌Triplet 5: 18 segments 5½″ wide

└Triplet 4: 18 segments 1½″ wide

TRIPLE-STRIP SET 4

Make 1 strip set for the table runner or the square lap quilt or 2 for the square full quilt. Subcut triplet 6.

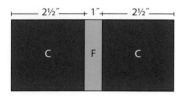

Table runner

—Triplet 6: 4 segments 2½" wide

Square lap quilt

—Triplet 6: 8 segments 2½" wide

Square full quilt

—Triplet 6: 18 segments 2½" wide

TRIPLE-STRIP SET 5

Make 1 strip set for the square lap quilt only (none for the table runner or the square full quilt). Subcut triplets 7 and 9.

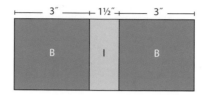

Square lap quilt

—Triplet 9: 8 segments 3" wide

—Triplet 7: 2 segments 2½" wide

TRIPLE-STRIP SET 6

Make 1 strip set for the square lap quilt only (none for the table runner or the square full quilt). Subcut triplet 8.

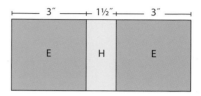

Square lap quilt

—Triplet 8: 5 segments 1" wide

TRIPLE-STRIP SET 7

Make 1 strip set for the square lap quilt only (none for the table runner or the square full quilt). Subcut triplets 10 and 11.

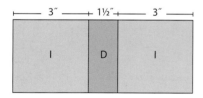

Square lap quilt

—Triplet 11: 4 segments 5½" wide

—Triplet 10: 4 segments 1½" wide

TRIPLE-STRIP SET 8

Make 1 strip set for the square lap quilt only (none for the table runner or the square full quilt). Subcut triplet 12.

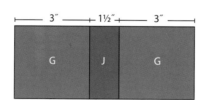

Square lap quilt

—Triplet 12: 4 segments 2½" wide

Connectors

Subcut connectors from the strips left over after you have made the strip sets.

FABRIC		CONNECTOR NUMBER	STRIP WIDTH	SUBCUT SEGMENTS THIS WIDE	QUANTITY		
					Table runner	Square lap quilt	Square full quilt
Green (B)		3	2½"	3"	16	16	24
		1	2½"	2½"	4	4	4
Yellow/green merge (E)		2	1"	2½"	10	10	14
Green/tan merge (I)		8	3"	5½"	16	32	48
		5	2½"	5½"	12	16	20
		4	2½"	1½"	8	8	12
Green/black merge (G)		6	2½"	2½"	8	8	12
Yellow/tan merge (H)		7	1"	5½"	10	20	28
Tan (D)		10	5½"	5½"	8	16	24
		9	5½"	1½"	8	16	24
Black/tan merge (J)		11	2½"	5½"	8	16	24

Making the Rows

Referring to the Row Types table for your quilt size (page 100), sew the triplets, quartets, and connectors together to make each type of row. To sew each row together, start with the piece listed at the left and add each segment in order from left to right. The numbers in each column refer to the triplet, quartet, or connector number you made in Triplets, Quartets, and Connectors (page 96). Refer to How to Build a Tartan Design, Step 5 (page 20) for detailed instructions on how to assemble the rows.

Row Types—Table Runner

ROW TYPE AND NUMBER TO MAKE	CONNECTOR	QUARTET	CONNECTOR	TRIPLET	CONNECTOR	INVERSE QUARTET	CONNECTOR
A: Make 2.	1	1	5	1	5	1	1
B: Make 5.	2	2	7	2	7	2	2
C: Make 8.	3	3	8	3	8	3	3
D: Make 4.	4	4	9	4	9	4	4
E: Make 4.	5	5	10	5	10	5	5
F: Make 4.	6	6	11	6	11	6	6

NOTE: Longer Table Runner

For a longer, three-pattern table runner, repeat rows 4–14 a second time, and end with the row A described for row 27.

Row Types—Square Lap Quilt

ROW TYPE AND NUMBER TO MAKE	CONNECTOR	QUARTET	CONNECTOR	TRIPLET	CONNECTOR	INVERSE QUARTET	TRIPLET	CONNECTOR	TRIPLET	CONNECTOR	INVERSE QUARTET	CONNECTOR
A: Make 2.	1	1	5	1	5	1	7	5	1	5	1	1
B: Make 5.	2	2	7	2	7	2	8	7	2	7	2	2
C: Make 8.	3	3	8	3	8	3	9	8	3	8	3	3
D: Make 4.	4	4	9	4	9	4	10	9	4	9	4	4
E: Make 4.	5	5	10	5	10	5	11	10	5	10	5	5
F: Make 4.	6	6	11	6	11	6	12	11	6	11	6	6

Row Types—Square Full Quilt

ROW TYPE AND NUMBER TO MAKE	CONNECTOR	QUARTET	CONNECTOR	TRIPLET	CONNECTOR	INVERSE QUARTET	QUARTET	TRIPLET	INVERSE QUARTET	QUARTET	CONNECTOR	TRIPLET	CONNECTOR	INVERSE QUARTET	CONNECTOR
A: Make 2.	1	1	5	1	5	1	7	1	7	1	5	1	5	1	1
B: Make 7.	2	2	7	2	7	2	8	2	8	2	7	2	7	2	2
C: Make 12.	3	3	8	3	8	3	9	3	9	3	8	3	8	3	3
D: Make 6.	4	4	9	4	9	4	10	4	10	4	9	4	9	4	4
E: Make 6.	5	5	10	5	10	5	11	5	11	5	10	5	10	5	5
F: Make 6.	6	6	11	6	11	6	12	6	12	6	11	6	11	6	6

Quilt Assembly

Referring to the quilt assembly diagrams (below and pages 102 and 103), sew the row types together in the indicated order to complete the quilt top. Press the seam allowances of each row in the opposite direction from adjacent rows. Pin at each and every seam intersection.

Row Number	*	Quartet	Connector	Triplet	Connector	Inverse Quartet	Triplet	Connector	Triplet	Connector	Inverse Quartet	*	Row Type
1	1	1	5	1	5	1	7	5	1	5	1	1	A
2	2	2	7	2	7	2	8	7	2	7	2	2	B
3	3	3	8	3	8	3	9	8	3	8	3	3	C
4	4	4	9	4	9	4	10	9	4	9	4	4	D
5	3	3	8	3	8	3	9	8	3	8	3	3	C
6	5	5	10	5	10	5	11	10	5	10	5	5	E
7	6	6	11	6	11	6	12	11	6	11	6	6	F
8	2	2	7	2	7	2	8	7	2	7	2	2	B
9	6	6	11	6	11	6	12	11	6	11	6	6	F
10	5	5	10	5	10	5	11	10	5	10	5	5	E
11	3	3	8	3	8	3	9	8	3	8	3	3	C
12	4	4	9	4	9	4	10	9	4	9	4	4	D
13	3	3	8	3	8	3	9	8	3	8	3	3	C
14	2	2	7	2	7	2	8	7	2	7	2	2	B
15	3	3	8	3	8	3	9	8	3	8	3	3	C
16	4	4	9	4	9	4	10	9	4	9	4	4	D
17	3	3	8	3	8	3	9	8	3	8	3	3	C
18	5	5	10	5	10	5	11	10	5	10	5	5	E
19	6	6	11	6	11	6	12	11	6	11	6	6	F
20	2	2	7	2	7	2	8	7	2	7	2	2	B
21	6	6	11	6	11	6	12	11	6	11	6	6	F
22	5	5	10	5	10	5	11	10	5	10	5	5	E
23	3	3	8	3	8	3	9	8	3	8	3	3	C
24	4	4	9	4	9	4	10	9	4	9	4	4	D
25	3	3	8	3	8	3	9	8	3	8	3	3	C
26	2	2	7	2	7	2	8	7	2	7	2	2	B
27	1	1	5	1	5	1	7	5	1	5	1	1	A

* Connector

Square lap quilt assembly -

Table runner assembly

Row Number	*	Quartet		Connector	Triplet		Connector	Inverse Quartet		*	Row Type
1	1	1		5	1		5			1	A
2	2	2		7	2		7			2	B
3	3	3		8	3		8			3	C
4	4	4		9	4		9			4	D
5	3	3		8	3		8			3	C
6	5	5		10	5		10			5	E
7	6	6		11	6		11			6	F
8	2	2		7	2		7			2	B
9	6	6		11	6		11			6	F
10	5	5		10	5		10			5	E
11	3	3		8	3		8			3	C
12	4	4		9	4		9			4	D
13	3	3		8	3		8			3	C
14	2	2		7	2		7			2	B
15	3	3		8	3		8			3	C
16	4	4		9	4		9			4	D
17	3	3		8	3		8			3	C
18	5	5		10	5		10			5	E
19	6	6		11	6		11			6	F
20	2	2		7	2		7			2	B
21	6	6		11	6		11			6	F
22	5	5		10	5		10			5	E
23	3	3		8	3		8			3	C
24	4	4		9	4		9			4	D
25	3	3		8	3		8			3	C
26	2	2		7	2		7			2	B
27	1	1		5	1		5			1	A

*Connector

Table runner assembly -------------------------------------

Square full quilt assembly

Row Number	*	Quartet		Connector	Triplet		Connector
1	1	1		5	1		5
2	2	2		7	2		7
3	3	3		8	3		8
4	4	4		9	4		9
5	3	3		8	3		8
6	5	5		10	5		10
7	6	6		11	6		11
8	2	2		7	2		7
9	6	6		11	6		11
10	5	5		10	5		10
11	3	3		8	3		8
12	4	4		9	4		9
13	3	3		8	3		8
14	2	2		7	2		7
15	3	3		8	3		8
16	4	4		9	4		9
17	3	3		8	3		8
18	5	5		10	5		10
19	6	6		11	6		11
20	2	2		7	2		7
21	6	6		11	6		11
22	5	5		10	5		10
23	3	3		8	3		8
24	4	4		9	4		9
25	3	3		8	3		8
26	2	2		7	2		7
27	3	3		8	3		8
28	4	4		9	4		9
29	3	3		8	3		8
30	5	5		10	5		10
31	6	6		11	6		11
32	2	2		7	2		7
33	6	6		11	6		11
34	5	5		10	5		10
35	3	3		8	3		8
36	4	4		9	4		9
37	3	3		8	3		8
38	2	2		7	2		7
39	1	1		5	1		5

Square full quilt assembly --------------------

Inverse Quartet		Quartet		Triplet	Inverse Quartet	Quartet	Connector	Triplet	Connector	Inverse Quartet	*	Row Type
1	7		1		7	1	5	1	5	1	1	A
2	8		2		8	2	7	2	7	2	2	B
3	9		3		9	3	8	3	8	3	3	C
4	10		4		10	4	9	4	9	4	4	D
3	9		3		9	3	8	3	8	3	3	C
5	11		5		11	5	10	5	10	5	5	E
6	12		6		12	6	11	6	11	6	6	F
2	8		2		8	2	7	2	7	2	2	B
6	12		6		12	6	11	6	11	6	6	F
5	11		5		11	5	10	5	10	5	5	E
3	9		3		9	3	8	3	8	3	3	C
4	10		4		10	4	9	4	9	4	4	D
3	9		3		9	3	8	3	8	3	3	C
2	8		2		8	2	7	2	7	2	2	B
3	9		3		9	3	8	3	8	3	3	C
4	10		4		10	4	9	4	9	4	4	D
3	9		3		9	3	8	3	8	3	3	C
5	11		5		11	5	10	5	10	5	5	E
6	12		6		12	6	11	6	11	6	6	F
2	8		2		8	2	7	2	7	2	2	B
6	12		6		12	6	11	6	11	6	6	F
5	11		5		11	5	10	5	10	5	5	E
3	9		3		9	3	8	3	8	3	3	C
4	10		4		10	4	9	4	9	4	4	D
3	9		3		9	3	8	3	8	3	3	C
2	8		2		8	2	7	2	7	2	2	B
3	9		3		9	3	8	3	8	3	3	C
4	10		4		10	4	9	4	9	4	4	D
3	9		3		9	3	8	3	8	3	3	C
5	11		5		11	5	10	5	10	5	5	E
6	12		6		12	6	11	6	11	6	6	F
2	8		2		8	2	7	2	7	2	2	B
6	12		6		12	6	11	6	11	6	6	F
5	11		5		11	5	10	5	10	5	5	E
3	9		3		9	3	8	3	8	3	3	C
4	10		4		10	4	9	4	9	4	4	D
3	9		3		9	3	8	3	8	3	3	C
2	8		2		8	2	7	2	7	2	2	B
1	7		1		7	1	5	1	5	1	1	A

* Connector

Gallery

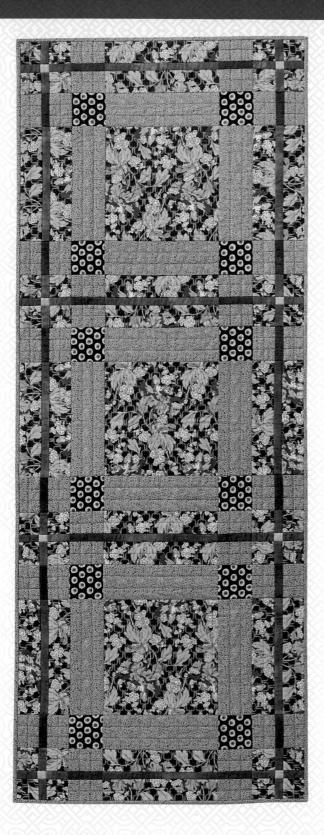

Elliot table runner, 25½″ × 67″, made by
Olive Lissner, quilted by Laurel Lissner, 2016

The traditional large-print blue floral used for the blue
background takes advantage of the large 10″ spaces in
the *Elliot* pattern. Despite the use of traditional fabrics,
this table runner has a very modern feel.

Elliot table runner, 25½″ × 67″,
made by Lola Thomas, quilted by
Shannon Ryan-Freeman, 2016

Made with Moda's Grunge line, Lola's table runner
is reminiscent of the traditional colors of the Elliot
tartan. The mottled fabrics give this quilt the look
of being handed down from mother to daughter
for generations.

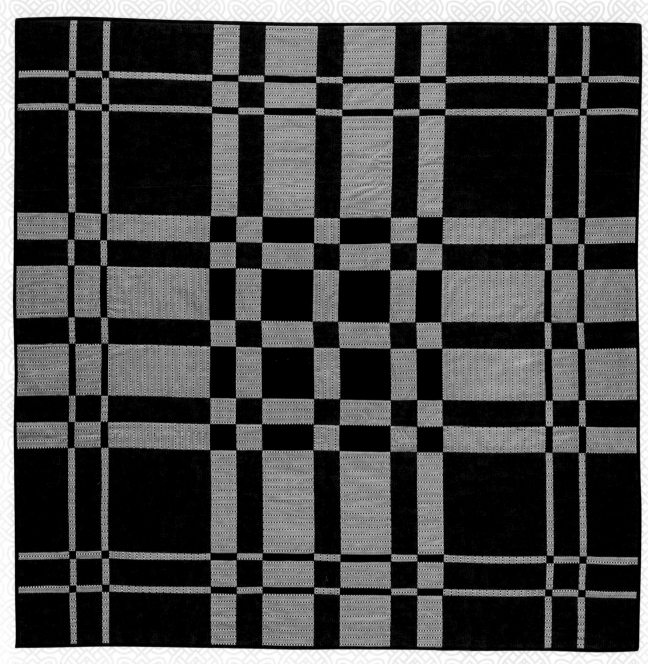

Maxwell sport lap quilt, 48″ × 48″, made and quilted by Cheryl Allen, 2016

Using a merge fabric with a white background—a lighter value than both base fabrics—makes the pattern stand out. Cheryl ignored the directionality of the merge fabric. The use of the light-value merge gives this quilt a dramatic effect.

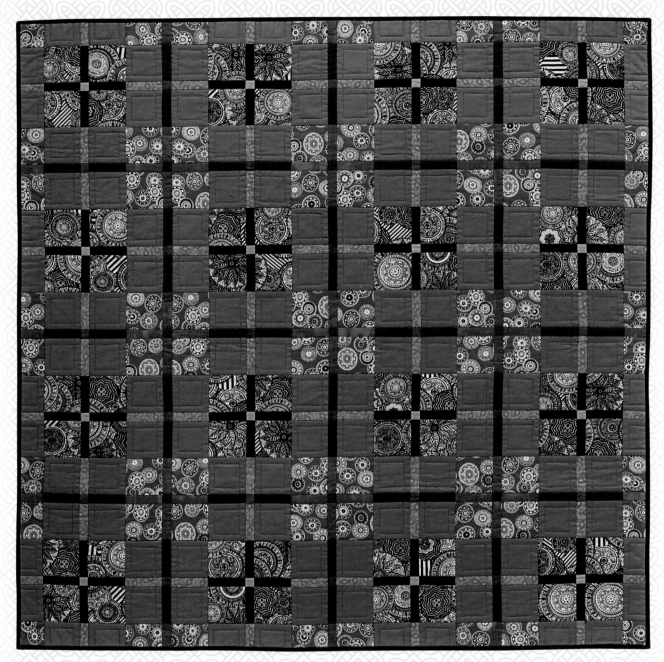

MacRae of Conchra square lap quilt, 51¼″ × 51¼″, made and quilted by Laurel Lissner, 2016

Laurel chose nontraditional fabrics for this quilt, substituting a gray-and-orange circular pattern for the traditional white and a low-value black-and-white circular pattern for the black. The multiple grays serve as a calm background, resulting in a stunning modern plaid.

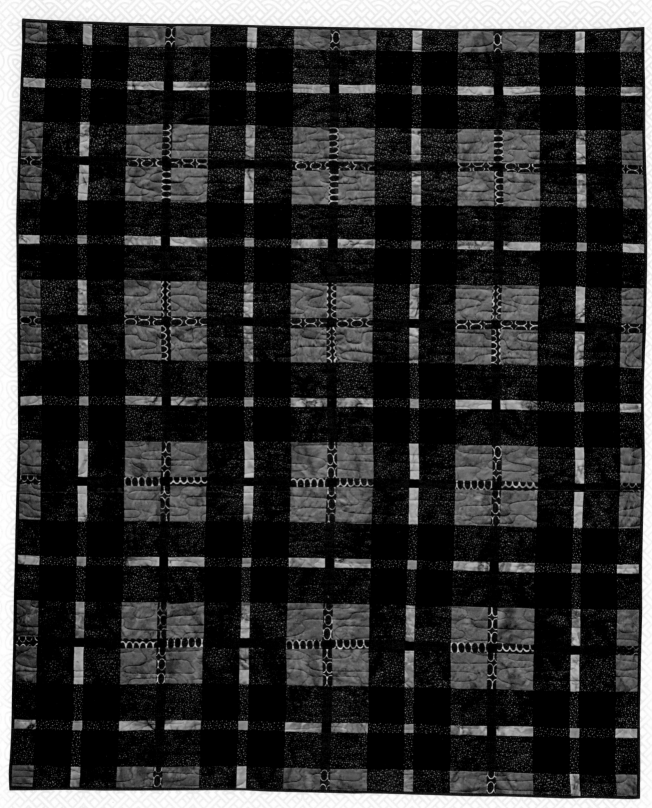

Modified *MacRae of Conchra* square lap quilt, 51″ × 62½″, made by Tricia Rogers, quilted by Shannon Ryan-Freeman, 2016

Tricia added a few extra rows to the small square lap quilt, making it perfect for a crib.
She replaced the white base color with bright blue, giving this quilt a cheery look.

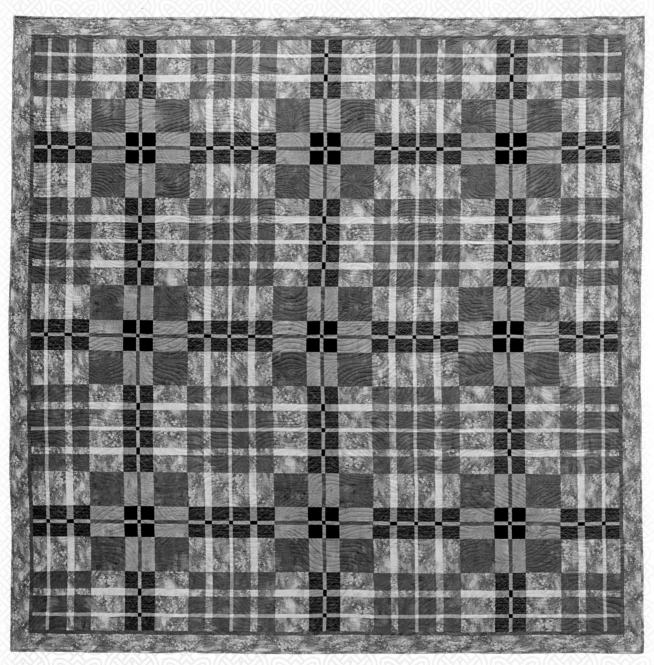

Amador square queen quilt, 90″ × 90″, made by Angel LeSage,
quilted by Shannon Ryan-Freeman, 2016

Angel's quilt is an excellent example of how changing the color combinations can result in a different look. She replaced some of the yellow and black base fabrics with the same purple fabric, making the tiny center the same color as the dissected four-patch at the center of each pattern. She also used the same fabric in some yellow/tan merge positions and for all yellow/black merge, giving the thin stripes a more consistent look. Finally, she used the base purple to replace some yellow/tan merge in the thin, bisecting stripes. Experimenting with fabric can provide stunning results.

Fabric Organization Worksheet
Keep track of your fabric choices by taping swatches next to the fabric colors.

FABRIC LETTER Write in the name of your fabric color (red, black, red/black merge).	FABRIC SWATCH Tape your fabric swatch in this column.
Fabric A	
Fabric B	
Fabric C	
Fabric D	
Fabric E	
Fabric F	
Fabric G	
Fabric H	
Fabric I	
Fabric J	
Fabric K	
Fabric L	
Fabric M	
Fabric N	
Fabric O	

About the Author

Kathy Allen started quilting in 2006, a little over a year after she retired from pharmaceutical project management. Trained in cell biology and toxicology, Kathy's work required travel throughout the United States, Canada, and Europe. Even while in the scientific world, Kathy was always drawn to quilts and fabric arts during her business travels.

Photo by Chris Axe

She and her sister-in-law enrolled in a local beginner's quilting class, and from that moment on Kathy was hooked. What started out as a hobby has become her passion. When she isn't quilting, Kathy studies history—in particular California's gold rush and the Kennedy Mine. In 2008, she prepared the written history for the National Park Service that put the Kennedy Mine on the National Register of Historic Places.

Kathy and her husband, Frank Axe, have spent a lot of the last decade traveling to Europe and throughout North America to view great architecture, visit friends, and study history. Ideas and inspiration for quilts come from these treks.

Kathy and Frank live and work in Sutter Creek, California. She currently designs and produces quilt patterns under the brand Quilts by Kat. She also keeps a blog about her travels and adventures in quilting.

Follow Kathy on social media:

Website: quiltsbykat.com

Facebook: /quiltsbykat

Bibliography

Banks, Jeffrey and Doria de la Chapelle. *Tartan: Romancing the Plaid.* New York, NY: Rizolli, 2015.

Collins Maps. *Tartans Map of Scotland.* London, UK: HarperCollins UK, 2012.

Collins Gem. *Clans & Tartans—A Guide to Tracing Both Clan and Tartan.* London, UK: HarperCollins UK, 2005.

Faiers, Jonathan. *Tartan.* London, UK: Berg, 2008.

Grimble, Ian. *Scottish Clans and Tartans.* New York, NY: Three Rivers Press, 1977.

Martine, Roddy. *Scottish Clan and Family Names.* Edinburgh, UK: Mainstream Publishing, 1996.

Scarlett, James Desmond. *Tartans of Scotland.* Cambridge, UK: Lutterworth Press, 1972.

Zaczek, Iain and Charles Phillips. *The Complete Book of Tartan.* London, UK: Lorenz Books, 2004.

Want even more creative content?

Make it, snap it, share it *using #ctpublishing*